Prentice Hall LITERATURE

PENGUIN EDITION

Unit Five
Resources

The British Tradition

PEARSON

Upper Saddle River, New Jersey
Boston, Massachusetts
Chandler, Arizona
Glenview, Illinois
Shoreview, Minnesota

13-digit ISBN: 978-0-13-366473-7
10-digit ISBN: 0-13-366473-2

1 2 3 4 5 6 7 8 9 10 12 11 10 09 08

CONTENTS

For information about the Unit Resources, a Pronunciation Guide, and a Form for Analyzing Primary Source Documents, see the opening pages of your Unit One Resources.

from **In Memoriam, A.H.H., "The Lady of Shalott,"**

from **The Princess: "Tears, Idle Tears," and "Ulysses"** by Alfred, Lord Tennyson

"My Last Duchess," "Life in a Love," "Love Among the Ruins," and "Porphyria's Lover" by Robert Browning

Sonnet 43 by Elizabeth Barrett Browning

"Progress in Personal Comfort" by Sydney Smith and Railroad Advertisement
by Thomas Cook

"Remembrance" by Emily Brontë

"The Darkling Thrush" and "Ah, Are You Digging on My Grave?"
by Thomas Hardy

"God's Grandeur" and "Spring and Fall: To a Young Child"
by Gerard Manley Hopkins

"To an Athlete Dying Young" and "When I Was One-and-Twenty"
by A. E. Housman

Writing Workshop: Historical Investigation 147

Writing Workshop: Transitions 148

Communications Workshop: Analyzing and Evaluating
Entertainment Media 149

Vocabulary Workshop 150

Essential Question Workshop 151

Benchmark Test 9 152

Diagnostic/Vocabulary in Context and Benchmark Test
Interpretation Guides. 158

Answers 162

Name _____

Concept Map Unit 5
Progress and Decline: The Victorian Period (1833–1901)

Three Essential Questions serve as lenses through which to view the literature—

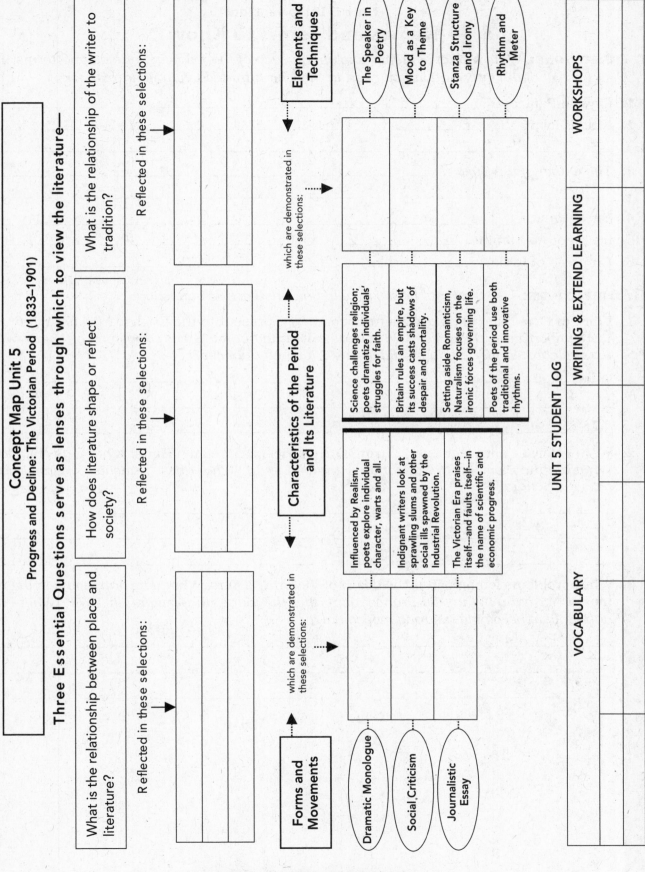

What is the relationship between place and literature?

Reflected in these selections:

How does literature shape or reflect society?

Reflected in these selections:

What is the relationship of the writer to tradition?

Reflected in these selections:

Forms and Movements

which are demonstrated in these selections:

- Dramatic Monologue
- Social Criticism
- Journalistic Essay

Characteristics of the Period and Its Literature

which are demonstrated in these selections:

Influenced by Realism, poets explore individual character, warts and all.

Indignant writers look at sprawling slums and other social ills spawned by the Industrial Revolution.

The Victorian Era praises itself—and faults itself—in the name of scientific and economic progress.

Science challenges religion; poets dramatize individuals' struggles for faith.

Britain rules an empire, but its success casts shadows of despair and mortality.

Setting aside Romanticism, Naturalism focuses on the ironic forces governing life.

Poets of the period use both traditional and innovative rhythms.

Elements and Techniques

which are demonstrated in these selections:

- The Speaker in Poetry
- Mood as a Key to Theme
- Stanza Structure and Irony
- Rhythm and Meter

UNIT 5 STUDENT LOG

VOCABULARY					WRITING & EXTEND LEARNING	WORKSHOPS

Name _____ Date _____

Names and Terms to Know

I. DIRECTIONS: *Write a brief sentence explaining each of the following names and terms. You will find all of the information you need in the Unit Introduction in your textbook.*

1. Crystal Palace: _____

2. King Edward VI: _____
   _____

3. *The Origin of the Species*: _____
   _____

4. Suez Canal: _____

5. Irish Potato Famine: _____

6. Empress of India*:* _____

II. DIRECTIONS: *Use the hints below to help you answer each question.*

1. What did the reign of Queen Victoria come to represent to the English? *[Hints: What values were important to the queen? What was celebrated in the Great Exposition of 1848? What was celebrated in Victoria's Golden and Diamond Jubilees?]*
   _____
   _____
   _____

2. What reforms were legislated during Queen Victoria's reign? *[Hints: What was child labor? What did the Elementary Education Act intend to do? What does "franchise" mean, and how was it extended?]*
   _____
   _____
   _____

3. What problems loomed after the death of Victoria? *[Hints: What was happening in the newly united Germany? What did France want after the war with Germany in 1871? Where was nationalism becoming a strong movement?]*
   _____
   _____
   _____

Name _____ Date _____

Unit 5 Introduction

Essential Question 1: What is the relationship between place and literature?

I. DIRECTIONS: *Answer the questions about the first Essential Question in the Introduction about the relationship between place and literature. All the information you need is in the Unit 5 Introduction in your textbook.*

A. *Extent of the British Empire*

  1. How much of the world was part of the British Empire at its height? _____

  _____

  2. What foreign nations had come under British rule? _____

  _____

B. *Spirit of Exploration and Conquest*

  1. What values were celebrated by Tennyson's hero Ulysses? _____

  _____

  2. How did these values differ from those of the medieval age, as represented by Dante's *Divine Comedy*? _____

  _____

C. *Literature Reflecting Empire*

  1. How was the ordinary British soldier portrayed in the poetry of Rudyard Kipling?

  _____

  2. What does Kipling's "Recessional" warn against? _____

II. DIRECTIONS: *Answer the questions based on the Essential Question Vocabulary words.*

  1. What might be the negative results of one people's *conquest* of another? _____

  _____

  2. Why might a country be proud of its ability to establish an *empire*? _____

  _____

  3. Why would someone near the end of life become concerned with the question of his or her *legacy*? _____

Unit 5 Introduction

Essential Question 2: How does literature shape or reflect society?

I. DIRECTIONS: *On the lines provided, answer the questions about the second Essential Question in the Introduction about the writer and social trends. All the information you need is in the Unit 5 Introduction in your textbook.*

A. *Best and Worst of Victorian Society*

  1. What positive attitude characterized the Victorian era, and what good results did this attitude achieve? _____

  _____

  2. What happened during the Irish Famine in the 1840s? _____

  _____

  3. What did the British army do to enemy families during the Boer War near the end of Victoria's reign? _____

B. *Wisdom and Foolishness*

  1. What scientific advances were made by Michael Faraday and Joseph Lister?

  _____

  2. What did the essays of Matthew Arnold urge his countrymen to do? _____

  _____

  3. What military folly was portrayed in Tennyson's "Charge of the Light Brigade"?

  _____

C. *Belief and Unbelief*

  1. What did the Victorians want to believe? _____

  2. What was the effect of the writings of Charles Darwin about evolution? _____

  _____

  3. What was paradoxical about the treatment of children during the Victorian age?

  _____

II. DIRECTIONS: *Complete the sentence stems based on the Essential Question Vocabulary words.*

  1. The *spirit* of the Victorian age is different from our own because _____

  _____

  2. *Modernization* can make life better by _____

  3. "It was the best of times; it was the worst of times" is a *paradox* because _____

  _____

Unit 5 Introduction

Essential Question 3: What is the relationship of the writer to tradition?

I. DIRECTIONS: *On the lines provided, answer the questions about the third Essential Question in the Introduction about the relationship between the writer and tradition. All the information you need is in the Unit 5 Introduction in your textbook.*

A. *Literature Looking Inward*

   1. What problem of his times does Tennyson address in "In Memoriam"? _____
_____

   2. What warning to his countrymen does Tennyson's *Idylls of the King* offer?
_____

B. *Sonnets and Dramatic Monologues*

   1. What Victorian notes does Elizabeth Barrett Browning add to the love sonnet? _____
_____

   2. What do the dramatic monologues of Robert Browning do? _____
_____

C. *The Victorian Novel*

   1. How were most Victorian novels published _____
_____

   2. Identify three prominent Victorian novels, along with one of their works. _____
_____

   3. What twin theme runs through much Victorian literature? _____

II. DIRECTIONS: *Answer the questions based on the Essential Question Vocabulary words.*

   1. How do you know when you are making *progress* in learning something? _____
_____

   2. Why would it be necessary to *reform* a system in which small children are sent to work to help support their families?
_____

   3. How could a novel provide a *commentary* about a social problem? _____
_____

   4. Under what circumstances might an ordinary person be called a *prophet*? _____
_____

Name _____ Date _____

Follow-Through Activities

A. CHECK YOUR COMPREHENSION: *Use this chart to complete the Check Your Comprehension activity in the Unit 5 Introduction. In the middle boxes, fill in a key concept for each of the Essential Questions. In the right boxes, fill in a key author relevant to each concept you list. (The second Essential Question has been done for you.)*

Essential Question	Key Concept	Key Author
Place and Literature		
Literature and Society	England as a world empire	Rudyard Kipling
Writer and Tradition		

B. EXTEND YOUR LEARNING: *Use this graphic organizer to help you prepare a multimedia presentation on the 1851 Crystal Palace and its displays.*

Research questions	Print source	Visuals / Sound source
What did the Crystal Palace look like?		
How was it constructed?		
What are examples of exhibits from England?		
From the Empire?		

Vocabulary Warm-up Word Lists

Study these words from the selections. Then, complete the activities.

Word List A

discerning [di SERN ing] *v.* perceiving or recognizing clearly
   As the year goes on, Mark is <u>discerning</u> his new job as quite satisfying.

feigned [FAYND] *adj.* not real; imagined
   Helen's <u>feigned</u> interest in Hector was meant to make Sam jealous.

idle [EYE duhl] *adj.* not busy
   My father is never <u>idle</u>, even though we urge him to slow down and relax.

remote [ri MOHT] *adj.* distant
   Carly is visiting a <u>remote</u> island for her vacation this year.

smite [SMYT] *v.* to strike or hit very hard
   Don used a heavy hammer to <u>smite</u> the nails that held the bench in place.

vexed [VEXT] *v.* irritated or annoyed
   The misbehaving child <u>vexed</u> the babysitter.

wanes [WAYNZ] *v.* grows progressively smaller in size or brightness
   The moon <u>wanes</u> for a few weeks and then slowly appears larger.

wrought [RAWT] *v.* formed or fashioned
   Years of wind and waves <u>wrought</u> changes on the shoreline.

Word List B

casement [KAYS muhnt] *n.* a window that opens as a door does
   Polly stood at the <u>casement</u> and looked up at the moon.

countenance [KOWN tuh nuhns] *n.* a face
   With a sorrowful <u>countenance</u>, Amy cuddled her sick puppy.

forecast [FOHR kast] *v.* to predict after studying available facts
   Meteorologists <u>forecast</u> the weather.

prosper [PRAHS per] *v.* to be successful; flourish; thrive
   Children <u>prosper</u> in a loving, secure environment.

prudence [PROO duhns] *n.* careful thought before acting
   Showing <u>prudence</u>, Jen did some research before buying the camera.

verge [VERJ] *n.* the edge of something; margin
   Long ago, people thought you could sail right off the <u>verge</u> of the earth.

yearning [YERN ing] *v.* to feel earnest longing or desire
   Kathryn, <u>yearning</u> for excitement, moved to New York.

yield [YEELD] *v.* to give up, as to superior power; surrender
   The general was determined not to <u>yield</u> to the enemy.

Poetry of Alfred, Lord Tennyson
Vocabulary Warm-up Exercises

Exercise A *Fill in each blank below with the appropriate word from Word List A.*

Jake and Andy play a game they call "Knights." Their interest in it waxes and

[1] _____. Some weeks, they play it a lot; other weeks, they don't. Lately,

they have been playing it often. It keeps them from being [2] _____.

"I'll [3] _____ you with this sword!" declares Jake with a

[4] _____ thrust at Andy's arm.

"You have [5] _____ me for the last time!" replies Andy,

fighting back with a rubber sword. Both swords, of course, have rubber tips so no one

can get hurt.

The sword that Jake uses is a finely [6] _____ weapon, an antique

that his grandfather's [7] _____ eye had picked out at a rummage sale.

Jake likes to imagine that it came from some [8] _____ country long ago.

Exercise B *Create two different sentences for each word in Word List B. You may use different forms of the vocabulary word for your second sentence.*

Example: Thunder storms were <u>forecast</u>. I cannot <u>forecast</u> who will win the games.

1. prosper:_____

_____

2. casement:_____

_____

3. countenance:_____

_____

4. verge:_____

_____

5. prudence: _____

_____

6. yearning:_____

_____

7. yield:_____

_____

Name _____ Date _____

Read the following passage. Pay special attention to the underlined words. Then, read it again, and complete the activities. Use a separate sheet of paper for your written answers.

Ulysses had been away from home for twenty years, traveling in <u>remote</u>, faraway lands; fighting in the Trojan War; and battling various monsters. Sometimes, he had thought he would never get home, especially when he and his men were trapped in the cave of the Cyclops, the one-eyed giant. Quick thinking and courage enabled Ulysses to <u>smite</u> the monster, blinding him with one hard blow and allowing his men to escape. Now, at last, he was back home and looking forward to relaxing with his wife, Penelope, and enjoying some <u>idle</u> hours doing nothing but resting.

However, it would not be as easy as he thought. While Ulysses was gone, Penelope had been <u>vexed</u> by various suitors who annoyed her daily. They insisted that her husband was dead and she should remarry. They refused to leave until she made a choice. With <u>feigned</u> sincerity, Penelope pretended she was interested in marrying one of them. She told them, "My hope for my husband's return <u>wanes</u>, growing weaker the longer he is gone. I will choose a new husband after I finish weaving a funeral robe for Laertes, my father-in-law."

Each day, she wove beautifully fashioned cloth at her loom. Each night, she undid the finely <u>wrought</u> designs she had made that day. You would think that even the least <u>discerning</u> eye would have recognized what was happening, but the suitors never caught on. Perhaps they were having too much fun living at Penelope's expense to say anything that might end the party.

Ulysses knew that he had to get rid of the suitors. His life would be in danger if they found out he had returned. In a mad frenzy, he and three friends managed to kill every last suitor. Finally, Ulysses was able to enjoy his own home.

1. Underline the word that means nearly the same as <u>remote</u>. Use **remote** in a sentence of your own.

2. Circle the words that give a clue to the meaning of <u>smite</u>. Write a definition for **smite**.

3. Underline the words that give a clue to the meaning of <u>idle</u>. What is an antonym for **idle**?

4. Circle the word that means nearly the same as <u>vexed</u>. Use **vexed** in an original sentence.

5. Circle the word that means nearly the same as <u>feigned</u>. Write a sentence of your own using **feigned**.

6. Underline the words that give a clue to the meaning of <u>wanes</u>. What is an antonym for **wanes**?

7. Circle the words that give a clue to the meaning of <u>wrought</u>. Describe a finely **wrought** tool or other item you own or would like to own.

8. Underline the words that give a clue to the meaning of <u>discerning</u>. Describe a piece of art or furniture that a **discerning** person might enjoy.

Poetry of Alfred, Lord Tennyson
Reading Warm-up B

Read the following passage. Pay special attention to the underlined words. Then, read it again, and complete the activities. Use a separate sheet of paper for your written answers.

One of the best-loved legends in British history is that of King Arthur and his Knights of the Round Table. No one knows how much of the legend is true, but King Arthur has come to symbolize an era in British history. According to the legend, Arthur invited the greatest and most chival-rous knights in all of Europe to Camelot, his castle. There they would thrive and <u>prosper</u> as part of Arthur's brilliant court in the early part of the sixth century. No one could have <u>forecast</u> that one of those knights would fall in love with the queen or predicted that it would bring about the fall of Camelot.

One can only imagine the young Queen Guinevere, married to the older Arthur but in love with young Sir Lancelot. She might be standing at a <u>casement</u> in the castle, looking out over the distant fields. The <u>yearning</u> expression on her face hints that she is longing to run away but is stopped by <u>prudence</u>, good judgment, and respect for her husband. Down on the ground, young Sir Lancelot, his sorrowful <u>countenance</u> revealing his deep love, might be looking up at her, waving good-bye as he leaves on one of his many quests.

According to the legend, Lancelot tried to stay away but eventually would <u>yield</u> to the temptation to see Guinevere. They were just on the <u>verge</u> of ending their relationship, about to say goodbye, when their love was discovered. Guinevere was sentenced to be burned at the stake, but Lancelot rescued her. In the process, he accidentally killed three of Arthur's allies, which started a war. The war ended when Arthur had to return to Camelot to stop a rebellion. Lancelot hurried to Camelot to help, but Arthur had already received a mortal wound, ending the dream that was Camelot.

1. Underline the word that means nearly the same as <u>prosper</u>. What do you have to do if you want a garden to *prosper*?

2. Circle the word that means nearly the same as <u>forecast</u>. Write an original sentence using *forecast*.

3. Circle the words that give a clue to the meaning of <u>casement</u>. Write a definition for *casement*.

4. Circle the word that means nearly the same as <u>yearning</u>. What is a synonym for *yearning*?

5. Underline the words that give a clue to the meaning of <u>prudence</u>. Tell about how you exercise *prudence*.

6. Circle the words that give a clue to the meaning of <u>countenance</u>. Describe the *countenance* of a person who has just received some very happy news.

7. Underline the word that tells what Lancelot would <u>yield</u> to. Write a definition for *yield*.

8. Underline the phrase that gives a clue to the meaning of <u>verge</u>. Use the word *verge* in a sentence.

Name _____ Date _____

from In Memoriam, A.H.H., "The Lady of Shalott," "Ulysses," and **from The Princess: "Tears, Idle Tears"** by Alfred, Lord Tennyson

Literary Analysis: The Speaker in Poetry

We can truly understand a poem only when we understand who is speaking and what motivated him or her to do so. In Tennyson's "Ulysses," the hero is an adventurer who not only reveals his longing to roam "with a hungry heart" but also attempts to persuade his aging followers and subjects that he and his band should leave the kingdom and "sail beyond the sunset."

DIRECTIONS: *On the lines, describe what Ulysses reveals in each quotation about his own thoughts and feelings or how he hopes to persuade his listeners with his words. Remember that both ordinary subjects and Ulysses's fellow adventurers are listening to him speak.*

1. How dull it is to pause, to make an end, / To rust unburnished, not to shine in use!

   _____

   _____

   _____

   _____

2. This is my son, mine own Telemachus, / To whom I leave the scepter and the isle / Well-loved of me, discerning to fulfill / This labor, . . .

   _____

   _____

   _____

   _____

3. . . . My mariners, / Souls that have toiled and wrought, and thought with me— / That ever with a frolic welcome took / The thunder and the sunshine, . . .

   _____

   _____

   _____

   _____

4. 'Tis not too late to seek a newer world. / Push off, and sitting well in order smite / The sounding furrows; . . .

   _____

   _____

   _____

   _____

Name _____ Date _____

from In Memoriam, A.H.H., "The Lady of Shalott," "Ulysses," and from The Princess: "Tears, Idle Tears" by Alfred, Lord Tennyson

Reading Strategy: Analyze Author's Assumptions and Beliefs

If we look beyond the words and images in poetry, we can often find the author's assumptions and beliefs. Depending on when and where the author lived and his or her experiences, those assumptions and beliefs may or may not be familiar to us. As you read a poem, first try to understand the speaker's meaning. The speaker may be the author of the poem or a fictional character. Once you understand what the speaker is saying, figure out the author's assumptions and/or beliefs that underlie the speaker's words.

DIRECTIONS: *In the following chart, record the poet's message and then what you believe to be the underlying assumption or belief in the message.*

Quote From Poem	Speaker's Meaning	Underlying Assumption/ Belief
1. But who shall so forecast the years/And find in loss a gain to match?/Or reach a hand through time to catch/ The far=off interest of tears? ("In Memoriam, A.H.H.")		
2. O Death in Life, the days that are no more. ("Tears, Idle Tears")		
3. I am a part of all that I have met;/ Yet all experience is an arch wherethrough/Gleams that untraveled world, whose margin fades/ Forever and forever when I move. ("Ulysses")		

from **In Memoriam, A.H.H.**, **"The Lady of Shalott," "Ulysses,"** and *from* **The Princess:**
"Tears, Idle Tears" by Alfred, Lord Tennyson
Figurative Language
Vocabulary Builder

A. DIRECTIONS: *Poems rely on figurative language to convey meaning in a fresh way. Underline examples of figurative language used in the following stanza from "In Memoriam, A.H.H." Write the literal and figurative meanings of two of the words you identify.*

Let Love clasp Grief lest both be drowned,
   Let darkness keep her raven gloss.
   Ah, sweeter to be drunk with loss,
To dance with death, to beat the ground

1. Word _____ Literal Meaning: _____ Figurative Meaning: _____
2. Word _____ Literal Meaning: _____ Figurative Meaning: _____

Using the Word List

chrysalis   churls   diffusive   furrows   prosper   prudence   waning

B. DIRECTIONS: *Choose the letter of the word or phrase most nearly* similar *in meaning to each numbered word. Write the letter of your choice in the blank.*

____ 1. diffusive
    A. polluted
    B. fervent
    C. dispersed
    D. alternate

____ 2. churls
    A. attitudes
    B. coarse persons
    C. emblems
    D. assigned duties

____ 3. waning
    A. bathing
    B. waxing
    C. expanding
    D. declining

____ 4. furrows
    A. grooves
    B. ponders
    C. plants
    D. lairs

____ 5. chrysalis
    A. flower bud
    B. cocoon
    C. soil
    D. crystal

____ 6. prosper
    A. sink
    B. play
    C. pretend
    D. thrive

____ 7. prudence
    A. carelessness
    B. carefulness
    C. haughtiness
    D. pettiness

Name _____ Date _____

from In Memoriam, A.H.H., "The Lady of Shalott," "Ulysses," and **from The Princess:
"Tears, Idle Tears"** by Alfred, Lord Tennyson

Integrated Language Skills: Support for Writing

Use the chart below to record information about Tennyson's life and poetry. Write events from Tennyson's life in each box in the left column in the order in which the events occured. Write his literary achievements in the boxes on the right. Then, circle the arrow that shows whether each literary achievement was an effect or a cause of the corresponding event in his life.

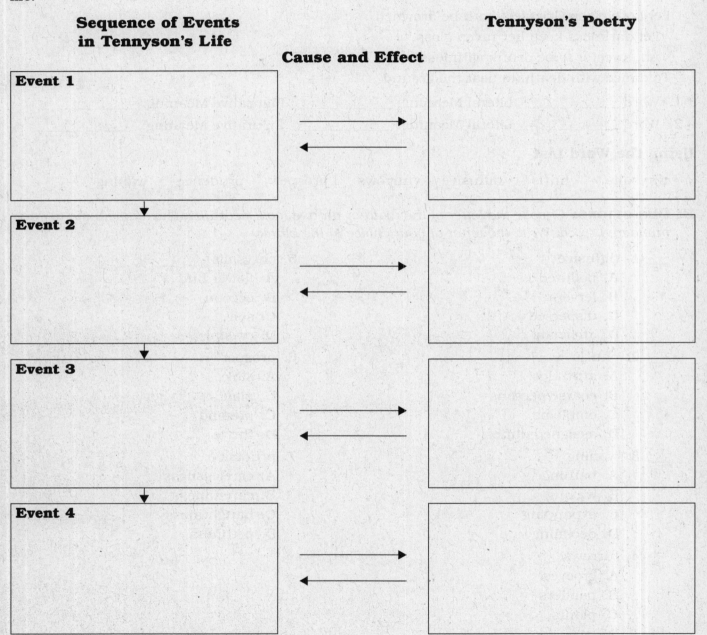

**Sequence of Events
in Tennyson's Life**

Tennyson's Poetry

Cause and Effect

Event 1

Event 2

Event 3

Event 4

On a separate page, use the information you have recorded in the chart as you write a draft of your biographical essay on Tennyson. Discuss the cause-and-effect relationship between his life and his work.

Unit 5 Resources: Progress and Decline
© Pearson Education, Inc. All rights reserved.
14

Name _____   Date _____

from In Memoriam, A.H.H., "The Lady of Shalott," "Ulysses," and from The Princess: "Tears, Idle Tears" by Alfred, Lord Tennyson

Enrichment: Culture

The role, practice, and expectations of education in the England of Tennyson's time differed greatly from what we are familiar with today. The few young men wealthy enough to attend school did not seek training in a career. Instead, they were introduced to a tradition for the cultivation of their minds and tastes.

The curriculum was heavily based on classical culture. Students took Latin and Greek, both grammar and literature. They read Horace and Aristotle for poetics; Julius Caesar and the Bible for history; the Greek tragedies, Homer and Virgil, Dante, Shakespeare, Milton, and others for literature. The astronomy of the time, as well as rudimentary mathematics, were sometimes part of the course of study, as was religion.

DIRECTIONS: *Fill out the following chart with information about your own curriculum. List the knowledge and skills each subject provides. Then, answer each of the questions that follow the chart.*

Subject	Knowledge/Skills Provided

1. What advantages might an education in the classical curriculum provide?

   _____

   _____

2. What are the primary advantages of a modern curriculum as opposed to those of a classical curriculum?

   _____

   _____

3. What remnants of the classical curriculum exist in modern subject areas?

   _____

   _____

4. What role might there be for some classical studies in the modern curriculum?

   _____

   _____

Poetry of Alfred, Lord Tennyson
Open-Book Test

Short Answer *Write your responses to the questions in this section on the lines provided.*

1. In "In Memoriam, A. H. H.," Tennyson expresses his grief over the death of a friend. Which line or lines from the poem best describe how he has come to terms with this loss?

   _____

   _____

   _____

2. Reread lines 9–16 of "In Memoriam, A. H. H." Analyze the poet's philosophical assumptions and beliefs, and compare them to your own observations and experiences. What is your evaluation of the poet's assumptions?

   _____

   _____

   _____

3. What is the theme of "In Memoriam, A. H. H."?

   _____

   _____

   _____

4. In "The Lady of Shallott," there is a part of the poem in which the speaker changes. Identify the line where the change occurs, and explain the effect that this change has on the poem.

   _____

   _____

   _____

5. Reread lines 58–63 from "The Lady of Shallott." How does the speaker of the poem view knights, and how does her view relate to the traditional concept of the behavior of a knight?

   _____

   _____

   _____

6. What is the philosophical belief about the relationship of artistry and loneliness that Tennyson tries to communicate in "The Lady of Shallott"?

   _____

   _____

   _____

7. In "Tears, Idle Tears," Tennyson expresses some ideas about how the world is perceived as people go through the different stages of life. Identify Tennyson's message by filling in the graphic organizer shown below.

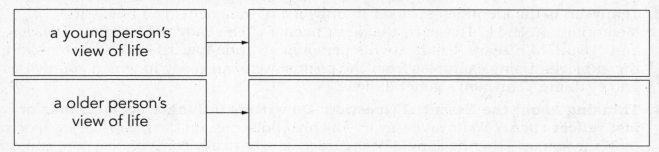

| a young person's view of life | → | |
| a older person's view of life | → | |

How would you evaluate Tennyson's message?

_____

_____

8. Who is the speaker of "Ulysses"? List quotations from the poem that indicate who the speaker is and what the speaker's conflict is.

_____

_____

_____

9. In "Ulysses," the speaker declares, "I am a part of all that I have met:/Yet all experience is an arch wherethrough/Gleams that untraveled world, whose margin fades/Forever and forever when I move" (lines 18–21). What does this quotation tell readers about what Ulysses is thinking?

_____

_____

_____

10. If the supply of something is *waning*, is it increasing or decreasing? Explain your answer.

_____

_____

_____

Essay

Write an extended response to the question of your choice or to the question or questions your teacher assigns you.

11. Think about the messages conveyed in each of Tennyson's poems: from *In Memoriam, A. H. H.,* "The Lady of Shallott," from *The Princess:* "Tears, Idle Tears," and "Ulysses." In an essay, tell which message you think is most meaningful to people today. Give reasons and examples to support your choice.

12. What happens to the Lady at the end of "The Lady of Shallott"? In an essay, answer this question, and explain how the Lady meets her fate. Include quotations or details from the poem that provide information about what happens to her.

13. Tennyson is the identified speaker in only one of the poems you read, "In Memoriam, A. H. H." However, the other poems—"The Lady of Shallott," "Ulysses," and "Tears, Idle Tears"—indicate his personal attitude toward his characters and the subjects. Using examples from the poems, write an essay in which you discuss and evaluate Tennyson's general ideas.

14. **Thinking About the Essential Question: Do writers influence social trends or just reflect them?** Write an essay in which you discuss, on the basis of these poems by Tennyson, whether he should be regarded as a basically conservative poet or as an innovative one. Support your main ideas with specific references to the text of the selections.

Oral Response

15. Go back to question 2, 4, 6, 7, 9, or the question your teacher assigns you. Take a few minutes to expand your answer and prepare an oral response. Find additional details in the selections to support your points. If necessary, make an outline to guide your oral response.

from In Memoriam, A.H.H., "The Lady of Shalott,"
from The Princess: "Tears, Idle Tears," and "Ulysses"
by Alfred, Lord Tennyson

Selection Test A

Critical Reading *Identify the letter of the choice that best answers the question.*

____ 1. What does Tennyson mean by "state to state" in these lines from *In Memoriam, A.H.H.*?
Eternal process moving on,
From state to state the spirit walks. . . .
   A. personal choices in life
   B. the end of life
   C. the stages of life
   D. different parts of the country

____ 2. What is the theme of *In Memoriam, A.H.H.*?
   A. The end of love is death.
   B. Love fails to prevent death.
   C. Death means an end to friendship.
   D. Love lasts even after death.

____ 3. Which answer choice best describes the speaker in *In Memoriam, A.H.H.*?
   A. a distant friend of A.H.H.
   B. Alfred, Lord Tennyson
   C. someone who did not know A.H.H.
   D. someone who worries over his own death

____ 4. Why did Tennyson write *In Memoriam, A.H.H.*?
   A. to honor a friend who died
   B. to celebrate Queen Victoria's reign
   C. to mourn the death of his father
   D. to describe a myth of long ago

____ 5. In "The Lady of Shalott," what does the Lady of Shalott spend her time doing?
   A. thinking
   B. waiting
   C. singing
   D. weaving

____ 6. What is one philosophical belief Tennyson tries to communicate in "The Lady of Shalott"?
   A. Society makes loners of artists.
   B. No one listens to poets.
   C. Love always ends unhappily.
   D. People should pay attention to curses.

_____ 7. What does the speaker mean in this line from "Tears, Idle Tears"?
   Dear as remembered kisses after death . . .

   A. The memory of kisses of someone who has died is sweet.
   B. Kisses we remember after we are dead are the dearest.
   C. We quickly forget the kisses of those who have died.
   D. We remember the kisses of only those who are now gone.

_____ 8. What is the main idea of "Tears, Idle Tears"?
   A. Mornings are a time of sad memories.
   B. People should be happy in the present.
   C. Memories cause sadness.
   D. All memories should not be sad.

_____ 9. Which term best describes the speaker in "Ulysses"?
   A. the poet
   B. fictional
   C. real
   D. generalized

_____ 10. What does the speaker plan to do in "Ulysses"?
   A. He plans to rule his country for many years.
   B. He plans to teach his son to be a good ruler.
   C. He plans to board his ship and sail away.
   D. He plans to retire and quietly await his death.

Vocabulary and Grammar

_____ 11. Which vocabulary word best completes this sentence?
   The ship dug temporary _____ in the sea as it sailed toward the west.

   A. diffusive
   B. churls
   C. waning
   D. furrows

_____ 12. Which word is an *antonym* for *waning* in these lines from "The Lady of Shalott"?
   In the stormy east wind straining,
   The pale yellow woods were waning . . .

   A. dying
   B. singing
   C. strengthening
   D. owning

_____ 13. Which of the following is an example of parallel structure?
   A. "Only reapers, reaping early / In among the bearded barley. . . ."
   B. "There she weaves by night and day / A magic web with colors gay."
   C. "And at the closing of the day / She loosed the chain, and down she lay . . ."
   D. "She left the web, she left the loom, / She made three paces through the room. . . ."

Essay

14. Think about the philosophical beliefs conveyed in each of Tennyson's poems: from *In Memoriam, A.H.H.*, "The Lady of Shalott," from *The Princess:* "Tears, Idle Tears," and "Ulysses." In an essay, tell which belief you think is most meaningful to people today. Give reasons and examples to support your choice.

15. "The Lady of Shalott" has been described as a poem about the loneliness of being an artist. Do you agree? Write an essay giving your opinion of this interpretation. Cite examples from the poem to support your opinion.

16. **Thinking About the Essential Question: Do writers influence social trends or just reflect them?** Based on the poems you read by Tennyson, is he a poet who is reflecting the traditions and ideas of his time, or is he an innovative poet, with new ideas to share? Write an essay discussing this question. In your answer, consider whether the following attitudes reflect the time in which Tennyson lived or seem more forward-thinking into present times: Tennyson's views on death, faith, artists and old age; the subject matter of Tennyson's poems; Tennyson's stylistic effects.

from **In Memoriam, A.H.H.,** **"The Lady of Shalott,"**
from **The Princess: "Tears, Idle Tears,"** and **"Ulysses"**
by Alfred, Lord Tennyson
Selection Test B

Critical Reading *Identify the letter of the choice that best completes the statement or answers the question.*

____ 1. "In Memoriam, A.H.H." was written by Tennyson to commemorate
    A. a dead close friend.
    B. the end of a love affair.
    C. sailors who died in a critical naval battle.
    D. the lives of common people.

____ 2. An author of a poem may communicate his own philosophical beliefs or assumptions
    A. only if he is speaking in his own voice.
    B. either in his own voice or in the voice of a fictional character.
    C. only if he has adopted the voice of a fictional character.
    D. only if he writes about his poetry in order to explain it.

____ 3. The speaker of "In Memoriam, A.H.H." seems to be
    A. a casual acquaintance of A.H.H.
    B. someone who never knew A.H.H.
    C. one who contemplates death impersonally.
    D. Tennyson himself.

____ 4. What is the meaning of the following line in "In Memoriam, A.H.H."?
    Far off thou art, but ever nigh

    A. The speaker regrets that A.H.H. ever left the country.
    B. No matter how much he remembers, death still removes his friend forever.
    C. Although A.H.H. is dead, the speaker holds his memory close.
    D. Death and life are closer than it may seem.

____ 5. What is the theme of "In Memoriam, A.H.H."?
    A. the endurance of love beyond death
    B. the tragic termination of friendship
    C. the awful injustice of dying young
    D. the gradual fading of painful memories

____ 6. In form and content, "The Lady of Shalott" recalls
    A. Christian allegories.
    B. national epics.
    C. medieval romances.
    D. classical drama.

_____ 7. Why may the Lady in "The Lady of Shalott" *not* leave her island?
   A. She has no means of transport at the poem's beginning.
   B. A curse is on her that forbids her to do so.
   C. The king in Camelot has forbidden her to do so.
   D. She is too overburdened with her weaving to do so.

_____ 8. One of Tennyson's underlying assumptions in "The Lady of Shalott" is the
   A. beauty of romantic love.
   B. social isolation of artists.
   C. danger of romantic love.
   D. sinister aspects of art.

_____ 9. In what way is the Lady in "The Lady of Shalott" like an artist?
   A. She suffers from a curse.
   B. She lives on a silent isle.
   C. She is robed in snowy white.
   D. She weaves a magic web.

_____ 10. Which of the following lines from "The Lady of Shalott" is the best evidence to support the poet's assumption that the Lady is doomed?
   A. "She knows not what the curse may be,"
   B. "She hath no loyal knight and true,"
   C. "She left the web, she left the loom"
   D. "There she weaves by night and day"

_____ 11. What is "Tears, Idle Tears" mostly about?
   A. the death of friends
   B. the futility of crying
   C. the pain of remembrance
   D. the horror of death

_____ 12. In "Tears, Idle Tears," when the speaker describes kisses that are "by hopeless fancy feigned," he means kisses that are
   A. secret.
   B. insincere.
   C. regretted.
   D. imagined.

_____ 13. In "Tears, Idle Tears," why does the poet describe the past as "Death in Life"?
   A. Events end and "die," and we experience that in life.
   B. The speaker's life no longer has meaning to him.
   C. Thoughts of death dominate the speaker's life.
   D. The past seems more alive than the present.

Vocabulary and Grammar

____ **14.** Parallel structure is the
   A. use of lines that are all more or less the same length.
   B. dispersal of thematic elements evenly throughout a work.
   C. balanced arrangement of stanzas in the sections of a narrative poem.
   D. use of repeated words, phrases, or grammatical forms.

____ **15.** In "The Lady of Shalott," what are these lines an example of?
   She left the web, she left the loom, / She made three paces through the room
   A. emotive language
   B. parallel structure
   C. foreshadowing
   D. onomatopoeia

____ **16.** A *furrow* is a _____.
   A. forehead
   B. ridge
   C. groove
   D. longboat

____ **17.** Things that are *waning* are _____.
   A. growing
   B. diminishing
   C. drenched
   D. enduring

Essay

18. In "Ulysses," an old man longs for one more chance to relive the glory of his youth. Write an essay in which you describe the nature of heroism the speaker of "Ulysses" hopes to display. Use specific examples from the poem to support your ideas.

19. Psychologists tell us that grieving for a loved one is a process in which a person goes through stages. In what sense does "In Memoriam, A.H.H." reflect such a process? Write an essay in which you explain how the poem progresses from one kind of feeling about death to others. Use examples from the poem to support your ideas.

20. **Thinking About the Essential Question: Do writers influence social trends or just reflect them?** Write an essay in which you discuss whether Tennyson should be regarded as a conservative poet or an innovative one. Support your answers with references to the underlying philosophy and beliefs in the Tennyson poems you have read.

Vocabulary Warm-up Word Lists

Study these words from the selections. Then, complete the activities.

Word List A

approving [uh PROOV ing] *adj.* accepting as good; regarding favorably
   With an <u>approving</u> smile, the mother watched her daughter practice ballet.

avowed [uh VOWD] *v.* declared; admitted
   Hana <u>avowed</u> that from this day forward, she would tell the truth.

pretense [PREE tens] *n.* a right or claim asserted with or without foundation
   The stranger made a <u>pretense</u> to the three brothers' inheritance.

pursue [per SOO] *v.* to try to find or get; strive for; chase after
   Bill chose to <u>pursue</u> his dream of becoming a doctor by studying hard.

spite [SPYT] *n.* a mean or bitter desire to annoy or harm someone else
   Angry with her brother, Beth broke his favorite video game out of <u>spite</u>.

trifling [TRY fuhl ing] *v.* to talk or act jokingly; deal lightly
   Barry felt that the mayor had been <u>trifling</u> with a serious matter.

vex [VEKS] *v.* to irritate or annoy; to cause worry; to be bewildering to
   Until I can remember his name, it is going to continue to <u>vex</u> me.

warily [WAIR uh lee] *adv.* in a watchful or cautious way
   Esther climbed the dark stairs <u>warily</u>, looking for the light switch.

Word List B

ample [AM puhl] *adj.* abundant; liberal
   This huge room has <u>ample</u> space for two beds and two dressers.

baffled [BAF uhld] *v.* puzzled; confused; bewildered
   Paulo, <u>baffled</u> by the difficult math problem, turned to Anar for help.

earnest [ER nist] *adj.* very serious; determined; sincere
   Edwin made an <u>earnest</u> plea for mercy, but the judge was not sympathetic.

exceed [ek SEED] *v.* to go beyond the limits of
   When fishing in this lake, you cannot <u>exceed</u> the limit of four fish.

ideal [eye DEE uhl] *adj.* perfect; excellent
   The house was built in an <u>ideal</u> location, overlooking the ocean.

prevail [pree VAYLE] *v.* to win or succeed; to be most common
   Superior free-throw shooting helped the team <u>prevail</u> against its rival.

rarity [RAIR uh tee] *n.* the condition of being uncommon or infrequent
   This large and perfect diamond is truly a <u>rarity</u> among gems.

sullen [SUL uhn] *adj.* showing bad humor or resentment; gloomy
   Not even the promise of ice cream could shake Ivan's <u>sullen</u> mood.

"My Last Duchess," "Life in a Love," and **"Porphyria's Lover"** by Robert Browning
"Sonnet 43" by Elizabeth Barrett Browning
Vocabulary Warm-up Exercises

Exercise A *Fill in the blanks, using each word from Word List A only once.*

Whenever I see my brother with that glum and [1] _____ expression on his face, I am completely [2] _____. After all, he seems to live in an [3] _____ world, so what does he have to be upset about? He has [4] _____ ability to achieve almost anything he wants to. He is that [5] _____ among men, a scholar-athlete. No matter the competition, either in sports or school, the team he is on will always [6] _____. I think that sometimes he feels that people's expectations of him [7] _____ his talents. Since he is so [8] _____ and responsible, he hates to let anyone down.

Exercise B *Revise each sentence so that the underlined vocabulary word is used in a logical way. Be sure to keep the vocabulary word in your revision.*

1. Before giving an <u>approving</u> response to a new dish, the chef makes sure the ingredients are stale.

   _____

2. With a big grin on his face, the toddler <u>warily</u> accepted the cookie.

   _____

3. To <u>pursue</u> a career in sports, it is important to lie around and watch television.

   _____

4. I will make a lot of noise while you're working so I won't <u>vex</u> you.

   _____

5. Shawn <u>avowed</u> his innocence, so he was punished for his actions.

   _____

6. I make no <u>pretense</u> at being an expert, but I know everything about art.

   _____

7. By <u>trifling</u> with Janelle's feelings, you will make her very happy.

   _____

8. To <u>spite</u> his neighbor, Hank helped him rake his leaves.

   _____

Name _____ Date _____

"My Last Duchess," "Life in a Love," and **"Porphyria's Lover"** by Robert Browning
"Sonnet 43" by Elizabeth Barrett Browning
Reading Warm-up A

Read the following passage. Then, complete the activities.

Many modern readers are quick to say they are <u>baffled</u> by poetry. They consider poetry a confusing and frustrating way to express an idea. Readers worry that they won't comprehend the figurative language that a poet uses, or that the structure of the phrases will <u>exceed</u> their ability to understand, leaving them bewildered.

At its origins, poetry is simply a way to pass down stories. In the earliest poems, the rhyming phrases and rhythmic patterns helped people memorize the words. Thus, it made it easier to take the information from village to village. In this way, epics such as *The Odyssey* were passed across miles and down through generations.

It is unfortunate that so many people avoid poetry. In fact, poetry can be the <u>ideal</u> art form to express emotions. For many poets, poetry is not only the best but the only way to bring a thought to life.

Understanding poetry may not come easily at first. It takes an <u>earnest</u> effort, not just a quick, insincere first reading. To really discover the layers of meaning in a poem may take time and thought. But it is worth the struggle to <u>prevail</u> and finally understand a poem.

Many people insist that they have never read poetry that they enjoy, and it is a <u>rarity</u> for them to find a poem that evokes a response. If people would abandon their <u>sullen</u> and negative attitude that poetry is a waste of time, they would surely be happily surprised to find an <u>ample</u> number of poets whose work impresses and inspires them.

1. Circle the words that give a clue to the meaning of <u>baffled</u>. Then write a sentence using the word *baffled*.

2. Underline the phrase that tells what readers are worried that poetry will <u>exceed</u>. Then give a word or phrase that means the same as *exceed*.

3. Circle the word that gives a clue to the meaning of <u>ideal</u>. Then underline the phrases that tell what poets think poetry is *ideal* for.

4. Underline the word that means the opposite of <u>earnest</u>. Then give a word or phrase that is a synonym for *earnest*.

5. Underline the phrase that tells what it will take to <u>prevail</u>. Then write a new sentence using the word *prevail*.

6. Underline the phrase that tells what some people think is a <u>rarity</u>. Give a word or phrase that means the same as *rarity*.

7. Circle the word that gives a clue to the meaning of <u>sullen</u>. Then circle the word that is an antonym for *sullen*.

8. Underline the phrase that tells what people will find an <u>ample</u> number of. Then give a word or phrase that means the opposite of *ample*.

"My Last Duchess," "Life in a Love," "Porphyria's Lover" by Robert Browning
"Sonnet 43" by Elizabeth Barrett Browning
Reading Warm-up B

Read the following passage. Then, complete the activities.

When Robert Browning met Elizabeth Barrett in 1845, the two poets could not <u>pursue</u> their courtship in an ordinary way due to some major obstacles. One big problem was that Elizabeth's father had <u>avowed</u> that none of his children should marry. So in order to marry Browning, Elizabeth would have to go against her father's declaration. As the eldest of her parents' twelve children, Elizabeth had no intention of <u>trifling</u> with their feelings. She took her parents' feelings seriously. But as an educated woman, she knew she had to make decisions about her life that might upset them. Robert and Elizabeth did not wish to <u>vex</u> her father, therefore their marriage the following year was, at least at first, a secret. Their union, after all, was based on genuine love and respect for each other, not on the desire to <u>spite</u> Elizabeth's father.

Within a year of their marriage, the Brownings moved to Florence, where they stayed for the rest of their married life. Their home in that city, which is known as Casa Guidi, now houses a library and museum dedicated to the poets. Today Casa Guidi has been lovingly restored and hosts events to encourage appreciation for the poets. The museum has a specific focus on the Brownings, and makes no <u>pretense</u> to be a complete source of information about the history of Florence.

Even those who usually approach poetry <u>warily</u>, because they are uncertain that they will understand it, find themselves having an <u>approving</u> reaction to Elizabeth Barrett Browning's poems. Sonnet 43, her best-known work, often leads to readers' nodding and smiling in recognition of the famous first line. A century and a half later, "How do I love thee? Let me count the ways," remains as clear and meaningful a statement as on the day it was written.

1. Underline the phrase that tells what Robert and Elizabeth wanted to <u>pursue</u>. Use the word *pursue* in a new sentence.

2. Underline the phrase that tells what Mr. Barrett <u>avowed</u>. Give a synonym for *avowed*.

3. Use clues in the passage to explain the meaning of <u>trifling</u>. Write a sentence using the word *trifling*.

4. Underline the phrase that tells what might <u>vex</u> Elizabeth's father. Give an example of something that might *vex* you.

5. Describe an action that might be designed to <u>spite</u> someone. Give a word or phrase that is a synonym for *spite*.

6. Underline the phrase that tells what the museum makes no <u>pretense</u> to be. Use *pretense* in a new sentence.

7. Circle the word that is a clue to <u>warily</u>. Give a word or phrase that means the opposite of *warily*.

8. Circle the phrase that gives a clue to the meaning of <u>approving</u>. Explain why readers might find themselves having an *approving* response to Browning's poems.

Name _____ Date _____

"My Last Duchess," "Life in a Love," and **"Porphyria's Lover"**
by Robert Browning
Sonnet 43 by Elizabeth Barrett Browning
Literary Analysis: Dramatic Monologue

A **dramatic monologue** is a speech, sometimes to a silent listener, in which a character indicates a setting and a dramatic conflict. In the monologue, this character reveals his or her inmost feelings, sometimes without knowing it.

A. DIRECTIONS: *Complete the following chart. Indicate the setting and names or general identities of the speaker and listener, and summarize the conflict in each poem.*

Poem	Setting	Speaker	Listener	Conflict
"My Last Duchess"				
"Life in a Love"				
"Porphyria's Lover"				

A **run-on line** ends where the flow of words forces you to read on without pause. An **end-stopped line** ends just where a speaker would naturally pause.

B. DIRECTIONS: *Identify which lines below are run-on lines and which are end-stopped lines.*

That's my last Duchess painted on the wall,   1. _____

Looking as if she were alive, I call   2. _____

That piece a wonder, now: Fra Pandolf's hands   3. _____

Worked busily a day, and there she stands.   4. _____

Name _____ Date _____

Reading Strategy: Compare and Contrast Speakers in Poems

The poems by Robert Browning and Elizabeth Barrett Browning all deal with the subject of love. However, each speaker has a distinct perspective on love.

DIRECTIONS: *Think about something or somebody you love. Use quotes below to compare and contrast each speaker's view and feelings about love to your own view and feelings about a person or thing that you love. If there is no comparison or contrast, say so, but make sure to explain.*

---

1. . . . Oh sir, she smiled, no doubt, / Whene'er I passed her; but who passed without/Much the same smile? This grew; I gave commands; Then all smiles stopped together.

↓

Speaker's view/feeling about love:

↓   ↓

This compares to my feelings about:	This contrasts with my feelings about:
Explain:	Explain:

---

2. I love thee with the breath,/ Smiles, tears, of all my life!

↓

Speaker's view/feeling about love:

↓   ↓

This compares to my feelings about:	This contrasts with my feelings about:
Explain:	Explain:

"My Last Duchess," "Life in a Love," and **"Porphyria's Lover"**
by Robert Browning
Sonnet 43 by Elizabeth Barrett Browning
Vocabulary Builder

Using the Suffix *-ence*

A. DIRECTIONS: *Answer each of the following questions, changing the underlined word to a word with the suffix* -ence.

1. Why was Alan <u>absent</u> from the meeting?

   _____

   _____

2. How did the class behave when there was an observer <u>present</u>?

   _____

   _____

3. Why did the teacher praise the <u>diligent</u> students?

   _____

   _____

4. How did the suspect prove he was <u>innocent</u> of the charge?

   _____

   _____

Using the Word List

countenance	dowry	eludes	minions	munificence
officious	sublime	sullen	vestige	

B. DIRECTIONS: *Match each word in the left column with its definition in the right column. Write the letter of the definition on the line next to the word it defines.*

___ 1. countenance

___ 2. officious

___ 3. munificence

___ 4. dowry

___ 5. vestige

___ 6. sublime

___ 7. minions

___ 8. eludes

___ 9. sullen

A. overly eager to please

B. state of being generous; lavishness

C. avoids or escapes

D. inspiring admiration through greatness or beauty

E. face

F. morose; sulky

G. natural talent, gift, or endowment

H. attendants or agents

I. trace; bit

"My Last Duchess," "Life in a Love," and **"Porphyria's Lover"**
by Robert Browning
Sonnet 43 by Elizabeth Barrett Browning

Integrated Language Skills: Support for Writing

You are a detective investigating the Duke's history and character for the father of a woman to whom the Duke has proposed. Use the cluster diagram to gather details from "My Last Duchess" about the duke's character and first marriage.

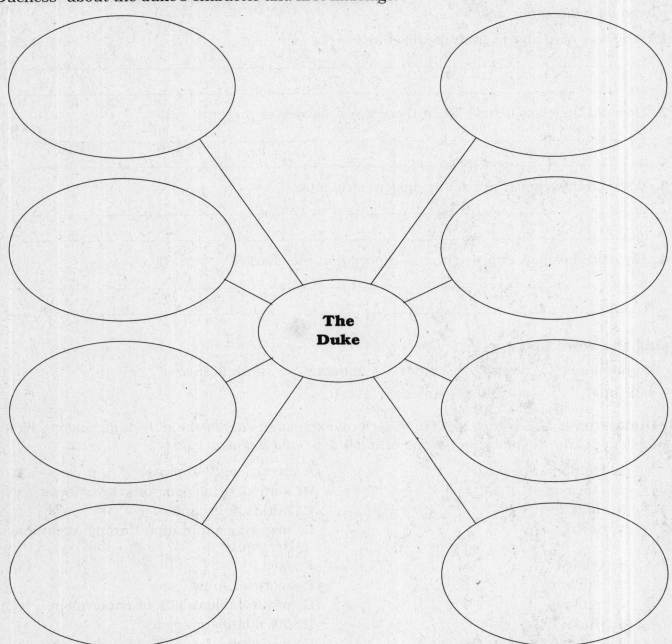

On a separate page, use the information you have gathered in your cluster diagram to help you draft a detective report for the woman's father about the duke's proposal. Start by presenting your position. Then, explain the reasons behind your position.

Unit 5 Resources: Progress and Decline
32

Name _____ Date _____

Enrichment: Fine Art

Reflections of a Poet's Theme

Like poets who can express a wealth of ideas in a concise form, artists can convey complex meaning in a single image. A piece of fine art accompanies two of the poems you read. These artworks are more than decorations; they reflect the poet's theme.

DIRECTIONS: *Complete the following chart by listing the main visual details and identifying lines from the poems that support those details. Then, draw conclusions about how each artwork reflects the poet's theme.*

Criteria for Analysis	*Antea* by Parmigianino and "My Last Duchess"	*La Pia de Tolommei* by Dante Gabriel Rossetti and "Porphyria's Lover"
Visual Details		
Related Lines from Poem		
Reflections of Poet's Theme		

33

Poetry of Robert Browning and Elizabeth Barrett Browning
Open-Book Test

Short Answer *Write your responses to the questions in this section on the lines provided.*

1. In Robert Browning's dramatic monologue "My Last Duchess," to whom is the Duke speaking? Explain your answer.

   _____

   _____

   _____

2. In "My Last Duchess," when the Duke refers to a gift he offered his last duchess (lines 33–34), why does he want his next duchess to appreciate it more fully, and why does he feel his "gift" is valuable?

   _____

   _____

   _____

3. How do you know that "My Last Duchess" is a dramatic monologue?

   _____

   _____

4. Reread lines 12–15 of "Life in a Love," and decide who or what strains the nerves, causes a fall, and takes up one's life. Explain your answer, using examples.

   _____

   _____

   _____

5. Use an example from "Life in a Love" to show how it works as a dramatic monologue, revealing the most intimate feelings of a single speaker.

   _____

   _____

   _____

6. Where does the turning point occur in the action the speaker describes in "Porphyria's Lover"? Explain your answer.

   _____

   _____

   _____

7. Give *two* examples of run-on lines in "Porphyria's Lover."

   _____

   _____

8. Use a Venn diagram to compare and contrast the character traits of the speakers in "My Last Duchess" and "Porphyria's Lover."

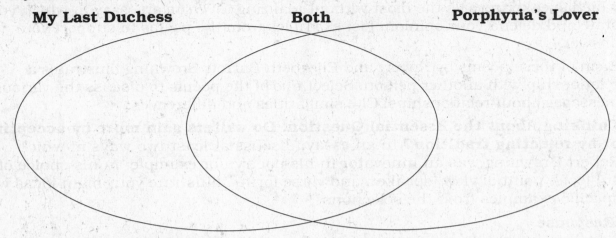

My Last Duchess   **Both**   **Porphyria's Lover**

Which speaker is presented more vividly, in your opinion? Explain your answer.

_____

_____

_____

_____

9. In Elizabeth Barrett Browning's "Sonnet 43," why do you think the speaker feels compelled to count the ways of romantically loving someone?

_____

_____

_____

10. If a person displays *munificence*, could he or she be described as generous or stingy?

_____

_____

_____

Essay

Write an extended response to the question of your choice or to the question or questions your teacher assigns you.

11. In an essay, briefly describe the type of person the Duke perceives his last duchess to have been in Robert Browning's "My Last Duchess." Use examples from the poem to support your description. Do you think the Duke is justified in thinking that his 900-year-old name deserves more respect?

12. The speakers in these poems express their feelings openly. However, they may not be aware of just how much they actually reveal about themselves. In your opinion, which speaker reveals the most without realizing it? Write an essay in which you state and defend your opinion. List examples from the poems to support your answer.

13. Each of these poems by Robert and Elizabeth Barrett Browning illustrates a relationship with another person. Select *two* of the poems to discuss the various messages about relationships. Cite similarities and differences.

14. **Thinking About the Essential Question: Do writers gain more by accepting or by rejecting tradition?** In an essay, discuss at least two ways in which Robert Browning was an innovator in his poetry: for example, in his choice of subjects, point of view, speaker, and verse forms. Illustrate your main ideas with specific examples from the selections.

Oral Response

15. Go back to question 2, 5, 7, 8, 9, or the question your teacher assigns you. Take a few minutes to expand your answer and prepare an oral response. Find additional details in the selections to support your points. If necessary, make an outline to guide your oral response.

Name _____ Date _____

"My Last Duchess," "Life in a Love," and **"Porphyria's Lover"** by Robert Browning
Sonnet 43 by Elizabeth Barrett Browning
Selection Test A

Critical Reading *Identify the letter of the choice that best answers the question.*

____ 1. Who is the speaker talking to in "My Last Duchess"?
A. his new wife, whom he has just married
B. his first wife, whose painting hangs on the wall
C. an agent for the father of the woman he wants to marry
D. himself, while he thinks about whom he wants to marry

____ 2. What is the subject of the speaker's monologue in "My Last Duchess"?
A. a portrait of his wife
B. the speaker's memory of his wife
C. the father of the woman he wants to marry
D. someone who wants to marry his wife

____ 3. When you compare the following two lines, what do the speakers have in common?
I gave commands;
Then all smiles stopped together.
("My Last Duchess")

Escape me?
Never—
("Life in a Love")

A. possessiveness
B. generosity
C. playfulness
D. eagerness to please

____ 4. How do you know "My Last Duchess" is a dramatic monologue?
A. The listener responds to the speaker's comments.
B. Both the speaker and listener address the reader.
C. The speaker is the person who wrote the poem.
D. The speaker addresses a silent listener.

____ 5. What is the main idea of "Life in a Love"?
A. Love is not worth the trouble or heartache.
B. Women have all the power in a relationship.
C. To be in love means to pursue your beloved.
D. Men do not know how to win a woman's love.

____ 6. Based on the description of the woman whom the speaker loves in "Life in a Love," how do her feelings compare to his?
A. She feels the same way he does.
B. She does not care for him.
C. She feels she has no chance of escape.
D. She hates him.

_____ 7. What do you learn about the speaker's mental state in "Porphyria's Lover"?
   A. He loves Porphyria and would do anything for her.
   B. He does not really love Porphyria.
   C. He loves someone else.
   D. He is mentally unstable.

_____ 8. In "Porphyria's Lover" there is a contrast between
   A. what Porphyria says and what she does.
   B. what the speaker says and what he does.
   C. the way each of the lovers feels about love.
   D. the stormy weather and the peaceful love.

_____ 9. In "Porphyria's Lover," what does the speaker use to strangle Porphyria?
   A. her hair
   B. his hair
   C. a rope
   D. a yellow string

_____ 10. Why does the speaker strangle Porphyria?
   A. to get revenge
   B. to hide his love
   C. the reader does not know
   D. he despises her

_____ 11. What question does the speaker answer in Sonnet 43?
   A. Does love survive death?
   B. In what ways do I love you?
   C. Do you love me?
   D. What is the meaning of love?

Vocabulary and Grammar

_____ 12. Which vocabulary word correctly completes this sentence?
   The crumbling tower was the only _____ that remained of a great civilization.
   A. countenance
   B. munificence
   C. vestige
   D. minion

_____ 13. Which sentence _incorrectly_ uses the italicized vocabulary word?
   A. His _officious_ smile assured her that his love would last.
   B. He declared his love, but her love still _eludes_ him.
   C. They watched the _sublime_ beauty of the setting sun.
   D. The king had _minions_ who stood ready to serve him.

____ 14. In which sentence is *like* or *as* used *incorrectly*?
  A. Robert Browning wrote the same type of poetry *as* Elizabeth did.
  B. Elizabeth Browning's style of writing is not exactly *like* that of her husband.
  C. Writers *like* Robert and Elizabeth Browning are rare.
  D. Some poets try to write just *like* Browning did.

Essay

15. Robert Browning's "Life in a Love" and Elizabeth Barrett Browning's Sonnet 43 are written about romantic love. In an essay, compare the intensity and strength of the love described in the two poems. How are the relationships that are described alike, and how are they different? Give examples and reasons to support your response.

16. In "Porphyria's Lover," the reader understands more about the speaker than he reveals about himself in his dramatic monologue. What is this information and how does the reader acquire it? What questions might the reader still have about the speaker?

17. **Thinking About the Essential Question: Do writers influence social trends or just reflect them?** Robert Browning was an innovator in his poetry in many ways. Where, traditionally, poets wrote about love, Browning adds an unexpected twist. Write an essay on how Browning handles the subject of love.

Name _____ . _____ Date _____

"My Last Duchess," "Life in a Love," and "Porphyria's Lover" by Robert Browning
Sonnet 43 by Elizabeth Barrett Browning

Selection Test B

Critical Reading *Identify the letter of the choice that best completes the statement or answers the question.*

____ 1. The speaker in "My Last Duchess" addresses
    A. no one.
    B. an artist painting a portrait.
    C. an agent representing a woman he wishes to marry.
    D. a sculptor he has hired to make a sculpture.

____ 2. How does the speaker in "My Last Duchess" compare to the Duchess herself?
    A. The speaker is weak and the Duchess was strong.
    B. The speaker is kind and the Duchess is unkind.
    C. The speaker and the Duchess are both loving.
    D. The speaker is powerful and the Duchess was vulnerable.

____ 3. "My Last Duchess" is considered a dramatic monologue because the speaker
    A. reveals himself through his own words.
    B. addresses his remarks to an absent person.
    C. discusses highly emotional issues.
    D. acts like a character in a play.

____ 4. What is the conflict in the dramatic monologue "Life in a Love"?
    A. The speaker must confess his lack of feeling for his beloved.
    B. The speaker suffers repeated rejections from his beloved.
    C. The speaker realizes he must find another love.
    D. The speaker is unable to tell his beloved of his feelings.

____ 5. What kind of speaker would have the opposite personality of that of the speaker in "Life in a Love?"
    A. a speaker who was in love
    B. a speaker who was beautiful
    C. a speaker who was confident
    D. a speaker who was not confident

____ 6. In "Porphyria's Lover" how does the speaker feel when Porphyria says she loves him?
    A. angry
    B. sad
    C. surprised and angry
    D. surprised and happy

____ 7. Where does the speaker get the yellow string to strangle Porphyria?
    A. from her hair
    B. the yellow string is her hair
    C. the poem does not say
    D. from his pocket

___ 8. What does the reader understand about the speaker from the speaker's contradictions?
   A. The speaker is old.
   B. The speaker is mentally unstable.
   C. The speaker is in love.
   D. The speaker is truly happy.

___ 9. The speaker strangles Porphyria
   A. because he does not love her.
   B. because he wants her to himself.
   C. but does not tell the reader why.
   D. but then wishes he did not do it.

___ 10. Sonnet 43 is mainly about
   A. the death of the speaker's beloved.
   B. the appearance of the speaker's beloved.
   C. the ways in which the speaker loves her beloved.
   D. the speaker's religious beliefs.

___ 11. In Sonnet 43, the speaker says,

   I love thee with a love I seemed to lose
   With my saints. . .

   A person who was very devout and valued religion over love would be

   A. the same as the speaker in Sonnet 43.
   B. the opposite of the speaker in Sonnet 43.
   C. the same as the speaker in Sonnet 43 because they both value religion most of all.
   D. different from the speaker in Sonnet 43 because she does not talk about religion.

___ 12. The theme of Sonnet 43 concerns the
   A. promise of life after death.
   B. obsessive quality of romantic love.
   C. difficulty of describing romantic love.
   D. transcendent value of romantic love.

Vocabulary and Grammar

___ 13. The source of his wife's happiness _____ the Duke.
   A. countenances
   B. officious
   C. minions
   D. eludes

___ 14. Despite his power and position, the Duke became jealous even when _____ paid attention to his wife.
   A. munificence
   B. dowry
   C. minions
   D. vestige

____ **15.** Hoping to win the woman's affection, the suitor demonstrated his _____ by sending her expensive gifts.
   A. countenance
   B. munificence
   C. dowry
   D. minions

On the line, write the letter of the one best answer.

____ **16.** Which sentence demonstrates the correct use of *like*?
   A. No one wrote dramatic monologues as well like Robert Browning.
   B. Sonnet 43 has fourteen lines like a sonnet should.
   C. I thought romances like theirs happened only in the movies.
   D. The ruins looked like they did in the photograph.

____ **17.** Poets _____ the Brownings were as well known in their time _____ today's entertainers.
   A. like; like
   B. as; as
   C. like; as
   D. as; like

Essay

18. Robert Browning is considered the master of the dramatic monologue. In an essay, analyze two of Browning's poems, explaining how they are examples of dramatic monologue and what they reveal about the speaker. Support your analysis with examples from the poems you choose.

19. The speakers in these poems profess their feelings openly. However, they may not be aware of just how much they actually reveal about themselves. In your opinion, which speaker reveals the most without realizing it? Write an essay in which you state and defend your opinion. Use examples from the poems to support your answer.

20. **Thinking About the Essential Question: Do writers influence social trends or just reflect them?** In an essay, discuss at least two ways in which Robert Browning was an innovator in his poetry—for example, in his choice of subjects, point of view, speakers, and verse forms. Illustrate your main idea with specific examples from the selections.

Vocabulary Warm-up Word Lists

Study these words from the selections. Then, complete the activities.

Word List A

contradiction [kahn truh DIK shun] *n.* denial; a statement that's the opposite of something
  In <u>contradiction</u> to his previous answer, Tony now said he could come to the party.

discard [dis KAHRD] *v.* to throw away, get rid of
  Be sure to <u>discard</u> the gum wrapper in the appropriate place.

dismal [DIZ muhl] *adj.* cheerless, gloomy; poorly performed
  The <u>dismal</u> weather kept us indoors all afternoon.

emphasized [EM fuh SYZD] *v.* stressed something as being important; made something stand out
  The judge <u>emphasized</u> his call for silence by banging the gavel.

feeble [FEE buhl] *adj.* physically or mentally weak; lacking strength
  Two weeks of fever left Rhonda <u>feeble</u> and tired.

immense [i MENS] *adj.* huge, extremely large
  An <u>immense</u> pile of snow blocked the entrance to the parking lot.

maim [MAYM] *v.* to wound someone very seriously
  Firecrackers have been known to <u>maim</u> people on the Fourth of July.

reign [RAYN] *n.* period during which a monarch, a royal power, or an authority rules a country
  The American Revolution took place during the <u>reign</u> of King George III.

Word List B

conviction [kuhn VIK shuhn] *n.* a belief that is fixed or firm
  His mother's <u>conviction</u> that he would do well gave Lebron confidence.

inflexible [in FLEK suh buhl] *adj.* rigid; stubborn; not able to be changed
  Mr. Carter had one <u>inflexible</u> rule: Students must treat one another with respect.

lustrous [LUS truhs] *adj.* shining, gleaming
  Vera polished the silver vase until it was <u>lustrous</u>.

nonsensical [nahn SEN si kuhl] *adj.* having little sense or meaning; silly
  Although the song's lyrics were <u>nonsensical</u>, the music was catchy.

objectionable [uhb JEK shun uh buhl] *adj.* offensive; causing disapproval
  The movie contained language that some viewers found <u>objectionable</u>.

representations [rep ri zen TAY shuhns] *n.* images or portrayals of something
  The paintings were supposed to be <u>representations</u> of the artist's emotions.

regulated [REG yuh lay ted] *v.* controlled by rules or laws; put in order
  The new rule <u>regulated</u> the students' use of athletic fields after school.

ventured [VEN churd] *adv.* did something in which risk was involved
  Davis finally got up his courage and <u>ventured</u> onto the freeway.

Name _____ Date _____

from **Hard Times** by Charles Dickens
Vocabulary Warm-up Exercises

Exercise A *Fill in the blanks, using each word from Word List A only once.*

Although we think of kings and queens as something from the distant past, monarchies still exist around the world today. In England, for example, although their political leaders are elected, a monarch continues to [1] _____ in Buckingham Palace. When the United States broke ties with England in 1776, the Founders thought that monarchy and democracy stood in [2] _____ to each other. They chose to [3] _____ the monarchy, and instead [4] _____ a system in which everyone is equal. This was an [5] _____ change, and it had a profound impact on the French, who soon overthrew their own royal family. Unfortunately for the French upper classes, revolutionaries there left a [6] _____ trail of violence and death. They saw their rulers as [7] _____ and useless, and used these views to justify their desire to [8] _____ or execute their rulers.

Exercise B *Decide whether each statement below is true or false. Circle T or F, and explain your answer.*

1. People who have the <u>conviction</u> that they're always right are easy to talk to.
   T / F _____

2. A teacher will usually praise a student for giving a <u>nonsensical</u> answer.
   T / F _____

3. A book that is <u>objectionable</u> to parents is always welcome in most classrooms.
   T / F _____

4. An <u>inflexible</u> opinion is difficult to change.
   T / F _____

5. A well-waxed car looks more <u>lustrous</u> in the sunlight.
   T / F _____

6. High school sports are <u>regulated</u> so that certain teams always win.
   T / F _____

7. An explorer who <u>ventured</u> into unknown waters might confront danger.
   T / F _____

8. Photos are two-dimensional <u>representations</u> of three-dimensional objects.
   T / F _____

from Hard Times by Charles Dickens
Reading Warm-up A

Read the following passage. Then, complete the activities.

During Queen Victoria's long <u>reign</u>, England underwent radical changes, including changes in the field of education. Schooling, which was previously only for the wealthy, began to be available to all children. Previously, the poor grew up unable to read or write. They were sent to work as soon as they were able, in order to help provide for their families. The <u>dismal</u>, bleak conditions in which they worked were an expected part of life for most children.

Victorian education <u>emphasized</u> a specific course of study. It stressed reading, writing, and arithmetic—known as the three Rs, based on the initial sound of each word. Repetition and memorization were key factors in a Victorian student's school day.

Classroom order was kept with strict discipline. It was not unusual for students to be struck with a cane or a ruler for an infraction of the rules. Teachers would never tolerate a student who disagreed with them or offered a <u>contradiction</u> to anything they said. Though perhaps the students were not beaten hard enough to <u>maim</u> them, it is not overstating the case to say that students received painful beatings on a regular basis.

Due to the <u>immense</u> expense involved, Victorian students did not write on paper and then <u>discard</u> their assignments in the trash when they were finished. Rather, they wrote on slates that could be wiped clean and then reused. For some lessons, boys and girls learned together. However, girls were considered too <u>feeble</u> of mind to handle the extra mathematics and science that the boys often studied. Instead, girls studied needlework and other household skills that they would most likely need later in life.

Victorian schools certainly bear little resemblance to their modern counterparts. Nonetheless, they represent an important step in the development of a universal system of education.

1. Circle the words that tell whose <u>reign</u> is described. Then, explain the difference between *reign* and *term*.

2. Circle the word that gives a clue to the meaning of <u>dismal</u>. Give a word that means the opposite of *dismal*.

3. Underline the phrase that tells what Victorian education <u>emphasized</u>. Use the word *emphasized* in a new sentence.

4. Circle the word that gives a clue to the meaning of <u>contradiction</u>. Then, give another word for *contradiction*.

5. Underline the word or phrase that gives a clue to the meaning of <u>maim</u>. Give a synonym for *maim*.

6. Circle the word that tells what was <u>immense</u>. Then, use the word *immense* in a sentence.

7. Underline the phrase that tells what Victorian students did not <u>discard</u>. Give a word or phrase that means the opposite of *discard*.

8. Circle the word that tells who was considered <u>feeble</u>. Give a synonym for *feeble*.

45

from **Hard Times** by Charles Dickens
Reading Warm-up B

Read the following passage. Then, complete the activities.

Charles Dickens was born well before the movies became a popular form of entertainment, but his stories seem to have been created for that medium. Start with his characters' names, for example. From the miserly Ebenezer Scrooge to the <u>nonsensical</u> and ridiculous Sweedlepipe and Pumblechook, Dickens invented names that brought his characters to life. Although fictional, these characters were exaggerated <u>representations</u> of the real people Dickens knew, and they remain fresh and interesting today.

Then there are his plots. Although there is violence and cruelty in Dickens's work, there is certainly nothing <u>objectionable</u> by the standards of today's movie-going public. Dickens was a social critic who used his writing to point out that under the <u>lustrous</u>, glowing exterior of the British Empire lurked poverty and despair. British readers may never have <u>ventured</u> into the grimy and dangerous parts of London that Dickens describes. But they didn't have to risk visiting these places themselves because Dickens's works opened their eyes to the terrible conditions around them.

Dickens was also concerned with the rigid laws and <u>inflexible</u> class structure that destroyed people's lives. His writing is credited with inspiring journalists and politicians to work to change them. Dickens knew about these issues firsthand. He worked in a factory 10 hours a day as a child after his father was thrown into prison for his debts. Dickens believed that there should be rules governing child workers. His <u>conviction</u> that working conditions should be <u>regulated</u> to protect children is a crucial theme in many of his works.

Starting as early as 1897, Dickens's characters and stories have come to life on the big and small screens and on stages around the world. Over a century after his death, Dickens remains a popular screenwriter.

1. Circle the word that gives a clue to the meaning of <u>nonsensical</u>. Write a new sentence using the word *nonsensical*.

2. Underline the phrase that tells what the characters were <u>representations</u> of. What else in Dickens's work might have been *representations* of something?

3. Use clues in the passage to explain the meaning of <u>objectionable</u>. How do people today know that a movie might have something *objectionable* in it?

4. Circle the word that means the same as <u>lustrous</u>. Give a word that means the opposite of *lustrous*.

5. Underline the phrase that gives a clue to <u>ventured</u>. Use the word *ventured* in a new sentence.

6. Circle the synonym for <u>inflexible</u>. Give an example of something that is *inflexible*.

7. Underline the phrase that tells what Dickens's <u>conviction</u> was. Explain the difference between *conviction* and *idea*.

8. Explain what Dickens thought should be <u>regulated</u>. Do you agree with him? Explain your answer.

Name _____ Date _____

from **Hard Times** by Charles Dickens
Charles Dickens, Biography

Charles Dickens, the widely read Victorian novelist, had a miserable childhood. He was left on his own while his father was in debtor's prison. The effects of his childhood lasted throughout Dickens's life and haunted him even after he had established himself as a writer, husband, and father. He wrote: *"My whole nature was so penetrated with grief and humiliation of such considerations, that even now, famous and caressed and happy, I often forget in my dreams that I have a dear wife and children; even that I am a man; and wander desolately back to that time in my life."* [source: http://www.pbs.org/wnet/dickens/pop_bio/index.html]

Imagine that you are Charles Dickens, and continue writing each of the following diary entries about important events in his life. Draw from the facts that you know about Dickens's life and use your imagination to fill in the details.

I cannot believe it! My father has been sent to debtor's prison and I am on my own.

I have just woken up from a nightmare, which is always the same.

It is only nine months since *The Pickwick Papers* was published, but boy, how my life has changed!

Name _____ Date _____

from **Hard Times** by Charles Dickens
Literary Analysis: The Novel and Social Criticism

A **novel** is a long work of fiction, usually featuring a complex plot, major and minor characters, a significant theme, and several settings. Like many novelists in nineteenth-century England, Charles Dickens created the fictional worlds in his novels to reflect real people and social institutions. Through his novels, he could comment on what he saw as problems and injustices in his society. This type of commentary through fiction is known as **social criticism.**

DIRECTIONS: *Examine the social criticism in* Hard Times *by answering the following questions.*

1. Of Thomas Gradgrind, Dickens writes: ". . . he seemed a kind of cannon loaded to the muzzle with facts, and prepared to blow [the students] clean out of the regions of childhood at one discharge." What is Dickens's attitude toward Thomas Gradgrind's teaching style? Why is this passage an example of social criticism?

   _____

   _____

   _____

2. When Mr. Gradgrind addresses student Sissy Jupe, he refers to her only as "girl number twenty." Why does he refer to her in this way? What viewpoint is Dickens criticizing by drawing attention to this? What aspect of the school is he criticizing?

   _____

   _____

   _____

3. Bitzer responds to a question about horses as follows: "Quadruped. Graminivorous. Forty teeth, namely twenty-four grinders, four eye teeth and twelve incisive. . ." What aspect of school is Dickens criticizing?

   _____

   _____

   _____

4. Dickens describes Mr. M'Choakumchild as one of "one hundred and forty other schoolmasters, had lately been turned out at the same time in the same factory, on the same principles like so many pianoforte legs." What is Dickens's opinion of teachers?

   _____

   _____

   _____

from **Hard Times** by Charles Dickens

Reading Strategy: Recognize the Writer's Purpose

A **writer's purpose** is his or her reason for writing a literary work. An author might write a novel for one or more of the following reasons: to address a social problem, to satirize a particular institution, or to entertain readers with humor or adventure. To understand a writer's purpose, pay close attention to the details he or she uses to describe characters, events, and ideas. These details reveal the writer's attitude, or feelings, toward what he or she is describing. The writer's attitude, in turn, suggests his or her purpose.

DIRECTIONS: *As you read the selection, try to determine the writer's purpose by answering the following questions.*

1. In Chapter 1 of *Hard Times,* what details does Dickens use to describe the schoolroom? What details does he use to describe the physical appearance of "the speaker" in the schoolroom? What might these details say about the author's attitude and purpose?

   _____

   _____

   _____

2. What details does Dickens use to create a contrast between Sissy Jupe and Bitzer? Why does Sissy clash with her teachers? What might the incident surrounding Sissy indicate about the author's attitude and purpose?

   _____

   _____

   _____

DIRECTIONS: *Write a short essay answering the following question:*

3. If Dickens's purpose had been to praise the educational system, many details in the story would be different. Choose a paragraph in the story and rewrite it here with different details to reflect the author's purpose of praising the educational system.

   _____

   _____

   _____

   _____

   _____

   _____

   _____

   _____

from **Hard Times** by Charles Dickens
Vocabulary Builder

Using the Prefix *mono-*

The Greek word prefix *mono-* means "single" or "alone." This meaning appears in *monotonous*, meaning "having a single tone" or "dull and unwavering."

A. DIRECTIONS: *Complete each sentence with a word shown below.*

monogram   monolithic   monophony   monosyllabic

1. The old library was a _____ stone structure.
2. His initials formed a _____ on his writing paper.
3. The song was a simple _____, without harmonizing parts.
4. The teacher repeated the _____ word *facts*.

Using the Word List

adversary   approbation   deficient   etymology
indignant   monotonous   obstinate   syntax

B. DIRECTIONS: *For each numbered word, choose the word that is most similar in meaning.*

___ 1. monotonous
   A. alone
   B. quiet
   C. exciting
   D. dull

___ 2. obstinate
   A. approving
   B. displeased
   C. stubborn
   D. slow

___ 3. adversary
   A. opponent
   B. partner
   C. student
   D. teacher

___ 4. indignant
   A. thoughtful
   B. displeased
   C. agreeable
   D. strict

___ 5. approbation
   A. punishment
   B. lesson
   C. approval
   D. plan

___ 6. deficient
   A. containing
   B. unfortunate
   C. lacking
   D. well-supplied

___ 7. etymology
   A. word study
   B. science of birds
   C. ecology
   D. historical study

___ 8. syntax
   A. sentence
   B. grammar
   C. word origins
   D. dictionary

Name _____ Date _____

from **Hard Times** by Charles Dickens
Grammar and Style: Avoiding Shifts in Verb Tense

The following is a list of **proper verb tenses** for the word "learn."

Present:	I learn
Past:	I learned
Future:	I will learn
Present perfect:	I have learned
Past perfect:	I had learned
Future perfect:	I will have learned

A. PRACTICE: *Correct the following sentences so that they avoid shifts in verb tense. Use the verb tense in parentheses in your rewritten sentence.*

1. Sissy learned that Mr. Gradgrind likes only facts and would not have appreciated original thought. *(past)*

   _____

   _____

2. The students in the class will grow up and understand that Mr. Gradgrind is wrong about his philosophy on education, and they will have lost respect for him. [future]

   _____

   _____

3. Bitzer appreciated the discussion on horses because it is amusing and it will distract the class from the math homework. [present]

   _____

   _____

B. Writing Application: *What is the most important thing for students to learn, and why? Write a short paragraph discussing your view of education. In your writing, use one of the "perfect tenses" and circle it.*

   _____

   _____

   _____

   _____

   _____

   _____

   _____

   _____

from **Hard Times** by Charles Dickens
Integrated Language Skills: Support for Writing

Use the chart below to record information about each source.

Bibliographic information for print sources should include the title, author's name, place of publication, publisher, and date of publication. Internet sources should have as much of the print information as you can find plus the Internet address and the date the site was researched.

Primary or Secondary	Bibliographic Information	Content and Comments

On a separate page, use the information in your chart to prepare your annotated bibliography. Include annotations that explain why each source was useful.

Name _____ Date _____

from **Hard Times** by Charles Dickens
Enrichment: Philosophy

Charles Dickens, in *Hard Times,* draws attention to the social issues and attitudes of England's Victorian period. In *Hard Times,* Dickens openly attacks some of the rigid ideals of Utilitarianism, a philosophy that influenced thought during this period. The basic beliefs of Utilitarianism philosophy include the following:

- Only what brings pleasure or makes future pleasure possible is good, or has usefulness. Usefulness can be calculated through logical, even mathematical, thought.
- All actions must be judged by their usefulness in promoting the greatest happiness for the greatest number of people. Governments must balance the interests of individuals against one another to make sure that happiness is maximized.
- The rightness or wrongness of an action is determined by its consequences, or outcome.

The founder of the first formal system of Utilitarianism was Jeremy Bentham, who first introduced the term in 1781. The ideas of Utilitarianism are based on his belief that the behavior of humans is driven by the wish to experience pleasure and avoid pain. He saw the need to instruct people on what pleasures were most beneficial to themselves and society— pleasures that endured, or that did not destroy the ability to enjoy other pleasures later. Thus, Utilitarianism emphasized not pleasure itself but usefulness, with the rational calculation of costs and benefits. Although many people, like Dickens, objected to Bentham's rigid attempts to calculate usefulness and human happiness, Bentham did bring about some positive changes in law and government. One of Bentham's most well-known followers, John Stuart Mill, used his belief in bringing about the "greatest good for the greatest number of people" to improve conditions for workers and the poor, and to try to bring about equality for women.

DIRECTIONS: *Answer each of the following questions.*

1. What are some positive aspects of Utilitarianism? Explain your answer and provide an example.

   _____

   _____

2. In what way is Thomas Gradgrind a model Utilitarian? What are the different ways in which he tries to promote "useful" conduct among his students? How does Dickens's portrayal of this character reflect his attitude toward Utilitarianism?

   _____

   _____

3. What are the negative aspects of Utilitarianism? Explain your answer and give an example.

   _____

   _____

   _____

from **Hard Times** by Charles Dickens
Open-Book Test

Short Answer *Write your responses to the questions in this section on the lines provided.*

1. What is the social issue that Charles Dickens addresses and criticizes in the excerpt from *Hard Times*?

   _____

   _____

   _____

   _____

2. Use the chart below to list the details in *Hard Times* that are clues to Dickens's purpose for writing the novel.

Subject of Excerpt and Ideas	Characters' Names	Dickens's Attitudes Toward Characters	Outcome

   Use the information to write a short statement summarizing Dickens's purpose.

   _____

   _____

   _____

   _____

3. Describe Thomas Gradgrind's teaching style as it is revealed in the excerpt from *Hard Times*.

   _____

   _____

   _____

   _____

4. Explain the significance of the "Facts" in the excerpt from *Hard Times*, and give a few details to support your explanation.

   _____

   _____

   _____

   _____

5. In the excerpt from *Hard Times*, Dickens refers to an "adversary." What is the meaning of this word? In the context of the final paragraph of the excerpt, who or what is the adversary being discussed?

_____

_____

6. In *Hard Times*, why does Mr. Gradgrind insist on calling Sissy Jupe "Cecilia"?

_____

_____

_____

7. What is Dickens's purpose in describing Mr. M'Choakumchild in this line?

> He and some one hundred and forty other schoolmasters, had been lately turned at the same time, at the same factory, on the same principles, like so many pianoforte legs.

_____

_____

_____

8. What is Dickens's object of social criticism in this excerpt from *Hard Times*?

_____

_____

_____

9. Why does Dickens have Gradgrind refer to Sissy Jupe as "girl number twenty"?

_____

_____

_____

10. How would you describe Dickens's overall tone in this excerpt from *Hard Times*?

_____

_____

_____

Essay

Write an extended response to the question of your choice or to the question or questions your teacher assigns you.

11. Suppose that you are a student in Mr. Gradgrind's class. Write a diary entry, from the point of view of either Sissy Jupe or Bitzer, about Mr. Gradgrind's teaching methods and your own experiences as one of his students. Be sure to make your entry consistent with Dickens's portrayal of the characters and the action in this excerpt from *Hard Times*.

12. The selection from *Hard Times* calls attention to two different students in Thomas Gradgrind's classroom: Sissy Jupe and Bitzer. How are these students different from each other? What specific details in the selection reveal these differences? What ideas does each character represent? What is the author's purpose in drawing attention to them in the selection? Discuss these questions in an essay.

13. In order to criticize the educational system in Victorian England, Dickens could have availed himself of other means. For example, he could have written a pamphlet, a letter to the editor, or a newspaper article. Why do you think that he chose the form of a novel for his criticism? What advantages, in terms of persuasive appeal to his audience, did this choice give the writer? Discuss these questions in an essay, supporting your main ideas with details from the selection.

14. **Thinking About the Essential Question: Do writers influence social trends or just reflect them?** In an essay, discuss the extent to which you think Dickens hoped for, or expected, substantial reform in the British education system. Use details from the excerpt from *Hard Times* to support your ideas.

Oral Response

15. Go back to question 2, 3, 4, 7, or the question your teacher assigns you. Take a few minutes to expand your answer and prepare an oral response. Find additional details in the selection to support your points. If necessary, make an outline to guide your oral response.

Name _____ Date _____

from **Hard Times** by Charles Dickens
Selection Test A

Critical Reading *Identify the letter of the choice that best answers the question.*

_____ 1. In *Hard Times*, what is the basis of Thomas Gradgrind's teaching?
A. Teach nothing but facts.
B. Encourage creativity.
C. Emphasize math and science.
D. Challenge students' imaginations.

_____ 2. What are the little "pitchers" in these lines from *Hard Times*?
Thomas Gradgrind now presented Thomas Gradgrind to the little pitchers before him, who were to be filled so full of facts.
A. teachers
B. books
C. students
D. notebooks

_____ 3. What does Mr. M'Choakumchild's name suggest about his teaching style?
A. He is a patient and gentle teacher.
B. He forces students to learn one way or another.
C. He wants to make sure that children learn facts.
D. He recognizes that students learn in different ways.

_____ 4. In *Hard Times*, why does Mr. Gradgrind insist on calling Sissy Jupe by the name Cecilia?
A. He misunderstands her when she first gives her name.
B. He thinks Cecilia is a prettier name than Sissy.
C. He cannot remember her real name and uses any name.
D. He thinks nicknames are silly and not to be used.

_____ 5. What is Dickens's purpose in describing Mr. M'Choakumchild in this line?
He and some one hundred and forty other schoolmasters, had been lately turned at the same time, in the same factory, on the same principles, like so many pianoforte legs.

A. He wants readers to know that a large number of musicians had recently become teachers.
B. He wants readers to know that many teachers were getting a thorough education.
C. He wants readers to know that teachers were all educated in exactly the same way.
D. He wants readers to know that teachers used imaginative techniques to reach their students.

_____ 6. What is Dickens's object of social criticism in this excerpt from *Hard Times*?
A. society's lack of emphasis on education
B. the lack of trained teachers and properly equipped classrooms
C. the indifference of teachers to their students' needs
D. a system of education that treats children like machines

____ 7. Dickens has Mr. Gradgrind call Sissy "Girl number twenty" to emphasize that
      A. there was an emphasis on mathematics in the classroom.
      B. he was oblivious to the individuality of students.
      C. he didn't like Sissy.
      D. there were only twenty students in the class.

____ 8. Dickens believes that a child's imagination
      A. is important and to be encouraged.
      B. gets in the way of more important facts.
      C. is to be used outside the classroom, only.
      D. distracts from serious learning.

____ 9. Dickens' purpose in writing *Hard Times* is to
      A. inform readers about a particular teacher.
      B. persuade readers to teach children more facts.
      C. entertain readers and share his criticism of the education system.
      D. entertain readers with a nonsensical story.

____ 10. What is Mr. Gradgrind's teaching style?
      A. flexible and creative
      B. rigid and hostile
      C. kind and forgiving
      D. unenthusiastic

____ 11. What kind of student is Bitzer, in Mr. Gradgrind's opinion?
      A. uncooperative
      B. average
      C. creative
      D. ideal

Vocabulary and Grammar

____ 12. Which vocabulary word correctly completes this sentence?
      Burns sat in a(n) _____ corner of the room where she would not be noticed and quietly read her book.

      A. monotonous
      B. obstinate
      C. indignant
      D. obscure

____ 13. Which sentence *incorrectly* uses a vocabulary word?
      A. Mr. Gradgrind looked his *adversary* straight in the eyes and demanded an apology.
      B. Students were encouraged to choose from the *approbation* of books on the shelves.
      C. Mr. Gradgrind insisted that the students use proper syntax.
      D. The *indignant* teacher straightened his waistcoat and stalked from the room.

____ 14. Which sentence contains an error in verb tense?

    A. Bitzer would have liked to learn that yesterday but he will learn it today instead.

    B. Sissy can have a carpet with flowers on it even though Mr. Gradigrind did not approve.

    C. Bitzer told Sissy the facts about horses and she smiles.

    D. Sissy still thought that horses could be very interesting and attractive animals.

Essay

15. In *Hard Times,* Dickens criticizes education without ever stating that he is doing so. Write a short essay describing something that you think is a problem without ever directly telling your reader your view of the subject. Make the problem clear by exaggerating the nature of the problem, as Dickens does in *Hard Times.*

16. Imagine that you are a student in Mr. Gradgrind's class. Write a journal entry as that student about your day in Mr. Gradgrind's classroom. You can be Sissy, Bitzer, or an imaginary student.

17. **Thinking About the Essential Question: Do writers influence social trends or just reflect them?** In *Hard Times,* Dickens is making a strong comment about the problems he sees in education. Do you think that in writing *Hard Times,* Dickens hoped to influence the educational system? In your answer, include a discussion of personal reasons that Dickens might have to want to change the educational system. Explain your answer.

from **Hard Times** by Charles Dickens
Selection Test B

Critical Reading *Identify the letter of the choice that best completes the statement or answers the question.*

____ 1. In *Hard Times,* on what principle is Thomas Gradgrind's teaching style based?
A. Teach gently but firmly.
B. Teach boys and girls to distinguish between facts and fancy.
C. Teach boys and girls nothing but facts.
D. Teach boys and girls to respect education and their elders.

____ 2. What is Dickens's purpose in describing Thomas Gradgrind as a "cannon loaded to the muzzle with facts" who will blow his students "clean out of the regions of childhood at one discharge"?
A. to reveal hatred of Gradgrind's inflexible and close-minded teaching style
B. to show Gradgrind's grasp of mathematics and basic facts
C. to encourage readers to admire Gradgrind's firm command of his classroom
D. to show Gradgrind's interest in the children he is teaching

____ 3. In *Hard Times,* who are the "little pitchers" waiting to be filled with facts?
A. imaginative students
B. teachers
C. all students
D. students interested in facts

____ 4. Why does Dickens have Gradgrind refer to Sissy Jupe as "girl number twenty"?
A. to criticize Gradgrind's inability to remember names and faces
B. to criticize the fact that students in the overpopulated school are treated as numbers, not individuals
C. to show readers the school's emphasis on mathematics
D. to take readers' attention away from individual students

____ 5. What is Dickens's purpose in describing the schoolmasters as being "turned out at the same time, in the same factory, on the same principles, like so many pianoforte legs"?
A. to show society's renewed interest in education and the proper instruction of teachers
B. to reveal his respect for educational institutions
C. to describe the training the teachers had to receive before teaching class
D. to attack the cold, mechanical nature of the teachers' approach to education

____ 6. What does Thomas Gradgrind's name suggest?
A. his dedication to his job as educator
B. his enjoyment of his students
C. the way he forces his ideas into the heads of his students
D. the way he molds children to be productive

_____ 7. In this selection from *Hard Times*, Charles Dickens is mainly criticizing
   A. the lack of respect young people have for education
   B. schools that smother imagination and treat children like machines
   C. schools that hire too many teachers
   D. schools that focus too much on discussion and not enough on reading and writing

_____ 8. Why does Dickens write that Mr. Gradgrind is "ready to weigh and measure any parcel of human nature, and tell you exactly what it comes to"?
   A. so that the reader will see Mr. Gradgrind is exact when he measures
   B. so that the reader will recognize that it is impossible to "weigh and measure" human nature
   C. to convey to the reader that Mr. Gradgrind is a devoted teacher
   D. to convey to the reader that Mr. Gradgrind loved math and science

_____ 9. What is Mr. Gradgrind's opinion of horse riders?
   A. He does not approve of them.
   B. He is fascinated with them.
   C. He believes they have a dangerous job.
   D. He believes they have an exciting job.

_____ 10. What is the purpose of Chapter 1 in the story?
   A. The author conveys the importance of facts.
   B. The author sets a scene that is boring and uncreative.
   C. The author sets a scene that is colorful and bright.
   D. The author discusses an important social issue.

_____ 11. What is the author's purpose in describing Bitzer as "so light eyed and light haired that the self-same rays appeared to draw out of him the little color he ever possessed"?
   A. to give readers a picture of what he looked like
   B. to paint Bitzer as a boring, colorless person
   C. to emphasize that he was light skinned
   D. to show that Bitzer had a superior attitude

_____ 12. Bitzer recites random irrelevant facts about horses to show that
   A. students can memorize important facts if they try.
   B. horses really don't matter.
   C. students are being taught irrelevant material.
   D. students are creative in their answers to questions.

_____ 13. What is Dickens's opinion of teachers who can answer "volumes of head-breaking questions"?
   A. They are not good teachers.
   B. They are good teachers.
   C. They are smart.
   D. They are creative.

_____ 14. What does Dickens think happens to students who are exposed to only factual learning?
A. They become well educated.
B. They become teachers.
C. They lose their creativity and individuality.
D. They gain creativity and individuality.

Vocabulary and Grammar

_____ 15. Which sentence is not in the present tense?
A. Sissy is wanting to use her imagination.
B. Sissy wants to use her imagination.
C. Sissy does want to use her imagination
D. Sissy will want to use her imagination.

_____ 16. Which sentence has an inconsistent tense?
A. Sissy will have been taught all the facts about horses.
B. Sissy will not have learned anything about life.
C. Mr. Gradgrind is wanting to have taught only facts' as he received training to do.
D. Dickens believed that teachers need to have better training and students need to be taught better.

_____ 17. Which is the best meaning of the word *truculent* as it is used in the sentence?
Jane spoke in a bitter and truculent manner when she was angry or excited.

A. harsh
B. polite
C. honest
D. loud

Essay

18. Write an essay comparing and contrasting the education you have received to the education described in *Hard Times*. Use specific examples to demonstrate differences and similarities.

19. **Thinking About the Essential Question: Do writers influence social trends or just reflect them?** In an essay, discuss the extent to which you think Dickens hoped for, or expected, substantial reform in the British education system. Use details from the excerpt from *Hard Times* to support your answer.

from **Hard Times** by Charles Dickens

from **Upheaval** by Anton Chekov

Literary Analysis: Comparing Social Criticism in Fiction

Social criticism in fiction is woven into a story and is not necessarily stated directly in the work, though sometimes it is stated through the thoughts, words, and actions of characters in the work. Social criticism in fiction often takes any of the following four forms:

1. The criticism is woven into a **realistic** story that shows life as it is to reveal social ills.

2. Social ills are **exaggerated,** which forces readers to see them more clearly.

3. The fictional story takes place in a **utopian,** or perfect, society to allow readers to draw conclusions about the ills in their own society.

4. The fictional story takes place in a **dystopian,** or dreadful, society, which leads readers to see what would happen if the social ills were allowed to continue.

DIRECTIONS: *Use the chart to compare and contrast the forms of criticism used in Dickens's and Chekhov's works.*

Hard Times by Charles Dickens

Social Criticism	How is it conveyed? (Quote from story or explanation)	Form (Realism; Exaggeration; Utopian; Dystopian)	Is there a character who sees the problem?
1.			
2.			

Upheaval by Anton Chekhov

Social Criticism	How is it conveyed? (Quote from story or explanation)	Form (Realism; Exaggeration; Utopian; Dystopian)	Is there a character who sees the problem?
1.			
2.			

Name _____ Date _____

from **Upheaval** by Anton Chekov
Vocabulary Builder

Using the Word List

ingratiating   kindred   palpitation   rummaging   turmoil

A. DIRECTIONS: *For each sentence, choose a word from the word list that best completes its meaning.*

1. Mashenka had no_____ who would take care of her when she left her job.

2. When Mashenka arrived, she found people _____ through her belongings.

3. Madame Kushkin was prone to heart _____s because of her nervous condition.

4. What was the use of all that work_____ herself to her employers if they would never trust her anyway?

5. The house was filled with _____ because of the missing brooch.

B. DIRECTIONS: *Match each word in the left column with its definition in the right column. Write the letter of the definition next to the word it defines.*

___ 1. turmoil

___ 2. rummaging

___ 3. kindred

___ 4. palpitation

___ 5. ingratiating

A. relatives

B. trying to win favor

C. upheaval

D. searching

E. rapid flutter of one's heart

from **Hard Times** by Charles Dickens

from **Upheaval** by Anton Chekov

Integrated Language Skills: Support for Writing

Chekhov and Dickens both use their fiction to criticize aspects of their societies. To compare the way each author gets his message across, the reader must first carefully analyze each selection's message and the way it is conveyed.

DIRECTIONS: *Use the graphic organizer below to help you organize your thoughts to write a compare-and-contrast essay about the means each author uses to convey his message.*

	Hard Times	*Upheaval*
1. Chief Social Criticism in the Selection		
2. Use of Realism? (If so, give examples.)		
3. Use of Satire? (If so, give examples.)		
4. Effectiveness of Social Criticism? (Give your opinion, with support.)		

TK

Name _____ Date _____

TK

Vocabulary Warm-up Word Lists

Study these words from the selections. Then, complete the activities.

Word List A

abyss [uh BIS] *n.* a bottomless space or gulf; anything extremely deep
At the canyon's edge, Barrett looked over the railing into the <u>abyss</u>.

commendations [kahm en DAY shuns] *n.* praise, approval
Liz received <u>commendations</u> from the mayor and the police for bravery.

crevices [CREV is ez] *n.* narrow cracks or openings
During the drought, <u>crevices</u> appeared in the dry lawn.

gleeful [GLEE fuhl] *adj.* full of joy; delighted
<u>Gleeful</u> laughter could be heard from the children's room.

merit [MER it] *n.* value; excellence; worth
Although his first book was poorly written, the second had some <u>merit</u>.

ominous [AHM uh nuhs] *adj.* threatening; menacing
An <u>ominous</u> silence preceded the explosion.

punctual [PUNK choo uhl] *adj.* strictly on time; prompt
Travis knew it was important to be <u>punctual</u> for his job interview.

retained [ri TAYND] *v.* kept hold of; remembered; hired
Ellie <u>retained</u> only random facts from the lecture.

Word List B

attained [uh TAYND] *v.* gained or reached; obtained
The minute he <u>attained</u> the age of 18, Johan registered to vote.

derived [di RYVD] *v.* received or obtained from a source
Vanilla extract is <u>derived</u> from vanilla beans.

dispense [di SPENS] *v.* give out; allot
Schools would <u>dispense</u> polio vaccine when it was first invented.

foresight [FAWR syt] *n.* planning for the future; seeing into the future
Thanks to the architect's <u>foresight</u>, the building withstood the earthquake.

passive [PAS iv] *adj.* not participating actively; putting up with something without resisting
Although the coach was shouting at her, Jenna remained calm and <u>passive</u>.

pensive [PEN siv] *adj.* thoughtful, often in a dreamy or sad way
Harwood looked at the sculpture with a <u>pensive</u> expression on his face.

restraint [ri STRAYNT] *n.* the state of being held back; limitation
Despite her anger, Mrs. Freeman showed <u>restraint</u> in her response.

vitality [vy TAL uh tee] *n.* great physical or mental energy
Even in his later years, Picasso showed a <u>vitality</u> that many younger people lack.

Name _____ Date _____

from Jane Eyre by Charlotte Brontë
Vocabulary Warm-up Exercises

Exercise A *Fill in the blanks, using each word from Word List A only once.*

As a child, Marcus approached the world with a [1] _____ smile. He was

always [2] _____, arriving in class well before the bell rang. Because he

took time with his papers, they usually had considerable [3] _____, and

he received more than his share of [4] _____ from teachers for his good

work. In high school, however, small [5] _____ began to appear in his

apparent perfection. Although for the most part he [6] _____ his positive

attitude, there were [7] _____ signs that could change at any moment.

Fortunately, his basic optimism led him to see that adulthood was not the frightening

[8] _____ that it seemed to be.

Exercise B *Circle the letter of the synonym, or word closest in meaning, to the vocabulary word.*

1. **passive**   a. inactive   b. rude   c. exhausted
2. **foresight**   a. foreground   b. forethought   c. forehand
3. **attained**   a. taught   b. helped   c. achieved
4. **vitality**   a. liveliness   b. loudness   c. suffering
5. **restraint**   a. repetition   b. limit   c. lesson
6. **pensive**   a. pondering   b. costly   c. written
7. **derived**   a. obtained   b. worn   c. grabbed
8. **dispense**   a. disagree   b. disturb   c. distribute

from **Jane Eyre** by Charlotte Brontë
Reading Warm-up A

Read the following passage. Then, complete the activities.

Julia stared at the blank page in front of her. The paper seemed so vast and empty that Julia felt she was looking into an <u>abyss</u>. Usually writing was a <u>gleeful</u> experience, the high point of her day, but for the past hour Julia had been unable to bring her story to a satisfactory conclusion.

Her writing, so vital to her, was nevertheless a secret from her family. She had been compelled to hide the manuscript, stuffing its pages into the <u>crevices</u> in the attic's unfinished walls. So far, the fissures in the wall had kept her work safe. Julia knew she would receive no <u>commendations</u> from her parents for her creativity. Rather, they would disapprove, and would be disappointed that their daughter shirked her household duties for such a frivolous activity. They saw no <u>merit</u> in a well-turned phrase or an imaginative plot twist. It was their belief, and, indeed, that of all society, that a well-raised girl should turn her fingers to needlework or piano practice, not the quill.

Suddenly Julia heard the <u>ominous</u> creaking of the bottom stair. Filled with dread, she had no doubt that the heavy tread belonged to her father. Julia, well practiced at hiding her hobby, quickly covered the evidence with a blotter and pulled out the tattered copy of *Jane Eyre*. She <u>retained</u> her composure, so she wouldn't look guilty and raise anyone's suspicions.

"Julia, have you forgotten the time? I expect my children to be <u>punctual</u> for meals," said her father in an annoyed tone.

"I was just coming down—but I just couldn't stop in the middle of the chapter," fibbed Julia. As she followed her father back downstairs, Julia breathed a quiet sigh of relief that her secret was safe for another day.

1. Circle the words that give clues to the meaning of <u>abyss</u>. Use the word *abyss* in a new sentence.

2. Underline the phrase that gives a clue to the meaning of <u>gleeful</u>. Give a word that means the opposite of *gleeful*.

3. Underline the phrase that tells where the <u>crevices</u> were. Give another word for *crevices*.

4. Circle the word that mean nearly the opposite of <u>commendations</u>. Give an example of an action that might receive *commendations*.

5. Underline the phrase that tells what held <u>merit</u> for Julia's parents. Give a synonym for *merit*.

6. Circle the word that tells what sound was <u>ominous</u>. Then, use the word *ominous* in a sentence.

7. Underline the phrase that tells what Julia <u>retained</u>. Give a word or phrase that means the opposite of *retained*.

8. Circle the word that gives a clue to the meaning of <u>punctual</u>. Give an antonym for *punctual*.

from **Jane Eyre** by Charlotte Brontë
Reading Warm-up B

Read the following passage. Then, complete the activities.

British novelist Charlotte Brontë published her first two novels under the pseudonym Currer Bell, a man's name. In doing so, she was part of a long tradition of women writers who hid their identity behind male names. In Brontë's day, women were still expected to be reserved, <u>passive</u> creatures who exhibited modesty and <u>restraint</u> in all their activities. It was considered unsuitable for women to write about characters who expressed strong feelings or showed <u>vitality</u> or independence. According to a book published in 1843, "a true lady is . . . sweet and delicate and refined." The man who chose to <u>dispense</u> this recommendation might have been shocked to learn that he was giving out such advice at a time when several favorite novelists were actually women.

Today, at least in Western countries, women have <u>attained</u> the same social status as men. Since they have reached equal status, women theoretically should not need to hide their names. Yet, there is still the suspicion that readers react differently to women writers than they do to men. The best-selling author J.K. Rowling, creator of the Harry Potter series, was told by her publisher that boys would not read books with a woman's name on the cover. Whether that prediction was shrewd <u>foresight</u> or not we will never know, since readers did not learn until after the first book's success that Rowling was female. By that time, they were hooked on the story. Readers <u>derived</u> such pleasure from following Harry's adventures that it didn't matter who the author was. Perhaps in <u>pensive</u> moments, Rowling wishes her first name, Joanne, adorned the covers of her books. It is likely that most of the time, she is too busy to think about that.

1. Circle the word that gives a clue to the meaning of <u>passive</u>. Give a word that means the opposite of *passive*.

2. Underline the word that gives a clue to the meaning of <u>restraint</u>. Use the word *restraint* in a new sentence.

3. Circle the phrase that gives a clue to the meaning of <u>vitality</u>. Give a synonym for *vitality*.

4. Circle the word that tells what the man chose to <u>dispense</u>. Explain the difference between *dispense* and *share*.

5. Underline the phrase that tells what women have <u>attained</u>. Use the word *attained* in a new sentence.

6. Circle the synonym for <u>foresight</u>. Do you agree with the publisher's decision? Explain your answer.

7. Underline the phrase that tells what was <u>derived</u> by Harry Potter readers. Give a synonym for *derived*.

8. Circle the word that gives a clue to the meaning of <u>pensive</u>. Use the word *pensive* in a sentence.

from **Jane Eyre** by Charlotte Brontë

Literary Analysis: Author's Political and Philosophical Assumptions

Everybody makes assumptions when they speak and when they write. Some of your assumptions are a product of where you live and the time period in which you live. For example, a woman in the Victorian era may assume that her place in society is less than that of a man. Much of what she says may contain this underlying assumption.

Example: *I couldn't wait for my husband to return home so that I could ask him if I could accept the invitation to the party.* The assumption in this sentence is that the husband is in charge of the wife's actions.

In a novel that contains social criticism, the author may make **political and philosophical assumptions** that are typical of the time in which he or she lives and may also make some **political and philosophical assumptions** that are new or different from the predominant ones at the time.

DIRECTIONS: *After each of the following quotes from the excerpt from* Jane Eyre, *record the political or philosophical assumption that underlies the statement.*

1. "Miss Smith put into my hands a border of muslin two yards long, together with a needle, thimble, etc., and sent me to sit in a quiet corner of the school room, with directions to hem the same."

   Assumption:

   _____

2. "Hardened girl!" exclaimed Miss Scatcherd, "nothing can correct you of your slatternly habits: carry the rod away."

   Assumption:

   _____

3. "Yes, in a passive way: I make no effort; I follow as inclination guides me. There is no merit in such goodness."

   Assumption:

   _____

4. ". . . like Felix, I put it off to a more convenient season."

   Assumption:

   _____

Name _____ · Date _____

from **Jane Eyre** by Charlotte Brontë
Reading Strategy: Analyze an Author's Assumptions

In a novel, an author's assumptions can be conveyed through characters, dialogue, and situations. In a novel that contains social criticism, some of the characters may reflect the "old system" that the author feels should be changed while others reflect the "new system," or the new ideas for change. When the reader examines the characters, dialogue, and situations, he or she can analyze them to understand both the author's assumptions and the philosophical and political ideas for change

DIRECTIONS: *Fill in the chart below to reflect the assumptions that Brontë makes in* Jane Eyre. *In the last column, decide whether Brontë approves of the assumption or feels it needs to change.*

Situation/Character/ Dialogue	Underlying Assumption	Brontë's Position
1. Helen Burns is subject to abuse by her teacher.		
2. " 'And if I were in your place, I should dislike her: I should resist her; if she struck me with that rod, I should get it from her hand; I should break it under her nose.' "		
3. "Helen's head, always drooping, sank a little lower as she finished this sentence."		
4. " ' . . . it is weak and silly to say you *cannot bear* what it is your fate to be required to bear.' "		

from **Jane Eyre** by Charlotte Brontë
Vocabulary Builder

A. DIRECTIONS: *Write a sentence with each of the vocabulary words. Make sure that your sentence shows that you know the meaning of the word.*

1. obscure:

_____

_____

2. comprised:

_____

_____

3. sundry:

_____

_____

4. tumult:

_____

_____

5. truculent:

_____

_____

Using the Word List

comprised   obscure   sundry

B. DIRECTIONS: *For each numbered word, choose the word that is most similar in meaning.*

___ 6. obscure
  A. vague
  B. correct
  C. clear
  D. lonely

___ 7. comprised
  A. organized
  B. taught
  C. argued
  D. contained

___ 8. sundry
  A. few
  B. angry
  C. ridiculous
  D. various

Name _____ Date _____

from **Jane Eyre** by Charlotte Brontë
Integrated Language Skills: Support for Writing

DIRECTIONS: *Reread the selection to find information you will need to write a school report on Helen Burns from the perspective of Miss Scatcherd. Use the charts below to record the information. Use this information to create your school report.*

Helen Burns

Schoolwork	
Effort	
Personal Hygiene	
Posture	

Ms. Scatcherd

Dialogue/ Actions	What it says about her character

Name _____   Date _____

from **Jane Eyre** by Charlotte Brontë
Enrichment: Film Production of *Jane Eyre*

Jane Eyre has been translated to film many times because of the richness of the story. Each adaptation brings its own interpretation and vision to Brontë's novel.

DIRECTIONS: *You are a filmmaker and are working on yet another version of* Jane Eyre *for film. But this time, you want to tell the story in the present day and adapt the story so that it is relevant to today's teenagers. Use the graphic organizer below to organize your thoughts about what new angle you might use for your film of the excerpt from* Jane Eyre.

Brief summary of the story:

What issues are the characters struggling with?

What similar issue might a modern teenager face?

Idea for film adaptation:

_____

_____

_____

Name _____ Date _____

from **Jane Eyre**, by Charlotte Bronte
Open-Book Test

Short Answer *Write your responses to the questions in this section on the lines provided.*

1. Briefly explain why Jane Eyre wants to talk to Helen Burns in the excerpt from Charlotte Brontë's novel, *Jane Eyre*.

   _____

   _____

   _____

   _____

2. Use the two-column chart below to explain the main differences between Jane's and Helen's ideas about what makes a good student.

Jane's Ideas	Helen's Ideas

   Which character do you think makes the more persuasive argument, and why?

   _____

   _____

   _____

   _____

3. Using the context of the excerpt from *Jane Eyre*, explain the meaning of the word *obscure*. How does Miss Scatcherd make it impossible for Helen Burns to remain obscure?

   _____

   _____

   _____

   _____

4. Use your own words to explain why Helen's thoughts do not wander when Miss Temple is teaching her.

   _____

   _____

   _____

   _____

5. In *Jane Eyre*, why do you think Brontë makes the cold bedroom, the meals, and the daily tasks part of the novel's setting?

_____

_____

_____

6. According to Helen Burns in *Jane Eyre*, why does Miss Scatcherd treat her so badly? What does this explanation suggest about Helen's character?

_____

_____

_____

7. How might you best describe the character of Helen Burns in *Jane Eyre*?

_____

_____

_____

8. In *Jane Eyre*, what does Helen's conversation with Jane reveal about the institution in which they live?

_____

_____

_____

9. Why do you think Charlotte Brontë chose to tell the novel *Jane Eyre* from the first-person point of view of Jane? What advantages does this choice afford the writer?

_____

_____

_____

10. Why is *Jane Eyre* considered a novel of social criticism? Briefly explain your answer.

_____

_____

_____

Essay

Write an extended response to the question of your choice or to the question or questions your teacher assigns you.

11. Helen and Jane have a long conversation near the end of the excerpt from *Jane Eyre*. In an essay, compare these two characters and their views of life and human nature. Are they more alike or more different? Use details from the selection to support your comparison.

12. Imagine that it is three years later, and you are either Jane Eyre or Helen Burns. You have not seen each other in some time. Write a letter from the point of view of the character of your choice. In your letter, discuss how your philosophy of life has matured. Be sure that your point of view and outlook are consistent with those of the characters portrayed by Charlotte Brontë in *Jane Eyre*.

13. Write an essay in which you describe the teaching styles of Miss Scatcherd and Miss Temple in this excerpt from *Jane Eyre*. Why does Helen think that Miss Scatcherd's style is better for her? What is your opinion?

14. **Thinking About the Essential Question: Do writers influence social trends or just reflect them?** In an essay, discuss how the contrast between the attitudes of Jane and Helen toward their teachers in the excerpt might reflect the contrast between the acceptance of social trends and a rebellion against them. Support your main ideas with specific references to the selections.

Oral Response

15. Go back to question 1, 2, 5, 6, 8, 9, 10, or the question your teacher assigns you. Take a few minutes to expand your answer and prepare an oral response. Find additional details in the selection to support your points. If necessary, make an outline to guide your oral response.

Name _____ Date _____

from **Jane Eyre** by Charlotte Brontë
Selection Test A

Critical Reading *Identify the letter of the choice that best answers the question.*

____ 1. What is Lowood in *Jane Eyre*?
   A. a summer school
   B. a public high school
   C. a girls' boarding school
   D. a wealthy family's home

____ 2. In *Jane Eyre*, why does Brontë describe the cold bedroom, the meals, and the daily tasks?
   A. to show the discomforts at Lowood
   B. to explain how education took place
   C. to show that life was interesting
   D. to reveal the courage of the girls

____ 3. What does Jane Eyre notice about Helen Burns as Jane is sewing?
   A. Helen is a good student.
   B. Helen is a poor student.
   C. Helen quietly accepts the teacher's constant criticism.
   D. Helen is constantly criticizing the teacher.

____ 4. What assumption is Brontë making about schools like the one Jane Eyre attends?
   A. They are a great opportunity for poor children.
   B. They deny children both respect and compassion.
   C. They are too expensive for families and society.
   D. They teach important skills but do not teach them well.

____ 5. What assumption does Miss Scatcherd make in *Jane Eyre* about the teacher/student relationship?
   A. Teachers may verbally and physically abuse students.
   B. Teachers may not verbally abuse students.
   C. Teachers may not physically abuse students.
   D. Personal hygiene is more important than learning.

____ 6. What assumption does Jane Eyre make that a modern-day student would also make?
   A. Sewing is a part of every girl's schoolday.
   B. Every student is well versed in the Bible.
   C. One must stand up for oneself against injustice.
   D. She must learn to be less rebellious.

____ 7. In *Jane Eyre*, what assumption underlies this quote: "Helen's head, always drooping, sank a little lower as she finished this sentence."
   A. A person who is constantly criticized is miserable.
   B. Students who are respectful keep their heads lowered.
   C. Helen is shy.
   D. Helen cannot look Jane in the eye.

____ 8. When Jane Eyre states "Burns made no answer: I wondered at her silence," Brontë's underlying assumption is
   A. students should be seen and not heard.
   B. students should mind their own business.
   C. Helen was not very bright.
   D. people should stand up for themselves.

____ 9. How are Jane Eyre and Helen Burns different?
   A. Jane is older, wiser, and more practical than Helen.
   B. Jane wants to fight injustices, but Helen quietly accepts them.
   C. Unlike Jane, Helen makes friends easily and is well liked by teachers.
   D. Jane is better at mathematics than Helen is.

____ 10. In *Jane Eyre*, Helen Burns has a _____ opinion of herself.
   A. healthy
   B. positive
   C. realistic
   D. negative

____ 11. Which student, Helen Burns or Jane Eyre, would be more likely to grow up and make change in the world?
   A. Jane Eyre
   B. Helen Burns
   C. both equally
   D. neither

Vocabulary and Grammar

____ 12. Which of the following vocabulary words from *Jane Eyre* correctly completes this sentence?

   When the curtain was drawn, it _____ Jane's view of Helen.

   A. comprised
   B. obscured
   C. tumulted
   D. sundried

____ 13. Which of the following vocabulary words from *Jane Eyre* correctly completes this sentence?

   Miss Scatcherd had a list of _____ complaints about Helen Burns.

   A. comprised
   B. sundry
   C. truculent
   D. tumult

_____ **14.** Which of the vocabulary words from *Jane Eyre* correctly completes this sentence?
Miss Scatcherd believes that Helen Burns is a _____ student.

    A. obscure
    B. sundry
    C. truculent
    D. tumult

Essay

15. Helen and Jane have a long conversation near the end of the excerpt from *Jane Eyre*. In an essay, compare and contrast these two characters and their views on life and human nature. Are they more alike or more different? Use details from *Jane Eyre* to support your answer.

16. Judging from your reading of *Jane Eyre*, what do you think Brontë saw as the problems with education in her time? In your answer, you may discuss the way the teachers treated their students, the attitudes of the teachers about what was important, and the expectations that everybody had about the students' conduct and learning. Cite specific examples from the selection to support your points.

17. Thinking About the Essential Question: Do writers influence social trends or just reflect them? In the excerpt from *Jane Eyre*, the contrast between the attitudes of Jane and Helen toward their teachers reflect the contrast between acceptance of social trends and rebellion against them. Write an essay about a social trend that affects you—for example, increasing communication on the Internet resulting in less face-to-face communication. Discuss what it would mean to accept the trend you choose and what it would mean to reject it. You may also examine whether there is a middle ground between complete acceptance and complete rejection.

from **Jane Eyre** by Charlotte Brontë
Selection Test B

Critical Reading *Identify the letter of the choice that best answers the question.*

____ 1. In *Jane Eyre,* what is Lowood?
   A. a summer camp for girls
   B. a strict boarding school for girls without title or money
   C. a program for privileged girls
   D. a school for both wealthy and poor girls

____ 2. What is the best way to describe Miss Scatcherd, as she is portrayed in *Jane Eyre*?
   A. understanding
   B. knowledgeable
   C. strict but supportive
   D. overly critical and cruel

____ 3. What is the author's underlying assumption about teachers like Miss Temple?
   A. A compassionate teacher is a good teacher.
   B. A compassionate teacher is not serious enough.
   C. Teachers must be strict to be effective.
   D. Some students don't respond well to compassion.

____ 4. How might you describe the character of Helen Burns in *Jane Eyre*?
   A. humble and dutiful
   B. unintelligent
   C. bitter and angry
   D. miserable

____ 5. According to Helen in *Jane Eyre,* why is Miss Satcherd severe with her?
   A. Miss Satcherd is evil.
   B. Miss Satcherd is a miserable person.
   C. Helen has many faults.
   D. Helen challenges Miss Satcherd too much.

____ 6. Jane Eyre wants to talk to Helen Burns because she
   A. thinks Helen is nice.
   B. believes Helen can help her sew.
   C. is curious about why Helen does not rebel.
   D. is curious about why Helen is not happy.

____ 7. In *Jane Eyre,* what is the main difference between Helen and Jane?
   A. Jane enjoys quiet reflection whereas Jane enjoys conversing.
   B. Jane is young and inexperienced whereas Helen is older and wiser.
   C. Jane dislikes learning whereas Helen loves learning.
   D. Jane wants to fight back at injustices whereas Helen quietly accepts them.

_____ 8. In *Jane Eyre*, what does Helen and Jane's conversation reveal about the institution in which they live?
   A. It encourages meditation and introspection.
   B. It places great value on learning.
   C. It denies people self-respect and individuality.
   D. It is a place where students work hard to better themselves.

_____ 9. In *Jane Eyre*, which character does Brontë identify with in terms of philosophical beliefs?
   A. Helen
   B. Jane
   C. Miss Scatcherd
   D. Miss Temple

_____ 10. In *Jane Eyre*, why does Brontë make the cold bedroom, the meals, and the daily task a part of the novel's setting?
   A. to show that Jane was ungrateful
   B. to show that Lowood was not a comfortable place
   C. to show that Helen had a reason to be homesick
   D. to show that the teachers were hungry and cold

_____ 11. In *Jane Eyre*, when Helen describes herself as having many faults, she shows an underlying lack of
   A. knowledge.
   B. self-confidence.
   C. creativity.
   D. imagination.

_____ 12. In writing *Jane Eyre* from Jane's point of view, Brontë is able to
   A. communicate with people who do not read well.
   B. make her characters and events more vivid, immediate, and realistic.
   C. make her characters and events more remote and historical, and therefore authentic.
   D. more easily communicate Helen's point of view.

_____ 13. How is *Jane Eyre* a novel of social criticism?
   A. It condemns educational practices at Victorian boarding schools.
   B. It condemns Lowood, a particular Victorian boarding school.
   C. It condemns a particular teacher at Lowood, a Victorian boarding school.
   D. It condemns a particular city and its schools.

_____ 14. After reading the excerpt from *Jane Eyre*, would you think Brontë would be in favor of today's laws against physical punishment for students at school?
   A. no
   B. yes
   C. unclear from the excerpt
   D. She would be in favor of it but would want very strict punishments to substitute for physical punishment.

Vocabulary and Grammar

____ 15. What is the best meaning of the word *truculent* as it is used in the sentence?

Jane spoke in a bitter and truculent manner when she was angry or excited.

A. harsh
B. polite
C. honest
D. loud

____ 16. What is the best definition of *sundry* as it is used in the following sentence?

The teacher complaints were a long list of sundry things that she thought Helen did wrong.

A. many
B. incorrect
C. obnoxious
D. diverse

____ 17. What is the best definition of the word *tumult* in the following sentence?

Jane's rebellious nature caused a tumult wherever she went.

A. peaceful situation
B. uproar
C. argument
D. problem

Essay

18. In *Jane Eyre,* what do Helen and Jane discuss? Write an essay describing their conversation and telling what the conversation reveals about the characters and their philosophies of life.

19. It is ten years after the events in *Jane Eyre.* You are either Jane Eyre or Helen Burns. Write a letter from the perspective of the character you choose to the other character, telling of your life as an adult. In your letter, discuss how your philosophy of life has matured. Be sure that your point of view and outlook are consistent with those of the characters portrayed by Brontë in *Jane Eyre.*

20. **Thinking About the Essential Question: Do writers influence social trends or just reflect them?** In an essay, discuss how the contrast between the attitudes of Jane Eyre and Helen Burns toward their teachers in the excerpt might reflect the contrast between the acceptance of social trends and a rebellion against them. Support your ideas with references to the selection.

Name _____ Date _____

James Berry Introduces "From Lucy: Englan' Lady," "Time Removed," and "Freedom"

DIRECTIONS: Use the space provided to answer the questions.

1. Briefly describe the author's roots, mentioned by James Berry in the first paragraph of his essay.

_____

_____

2. Why is Rudyard Kipling's poem "Recessional" significant for Berry?

_____

_____

3. According to Berry, what is Lucy's attitude toward the Queen of England? What does Lucy's outlook represent?

_____

_____

_____

_____

4. When James Berry returned to Jamaica after a long absence, how did he feel when he saw his homeland again?

_____

_____

5. According to Berry, how did England contrast with Jamaica?

_____

_____

_____

6. What explanation does Berry offer for the title of his poem "Time Removed"?

_____

_____

7. What seems to be Berry's attitude toward the pain and suffering of the past? How do you evaluate this attitude? Briefly explain your answer.

_____

_____

_____

_____

James Berry
Listening and Viewing

Segment 1: Meet James Berry
- As a young boy, how did James Berry use his interests as the basis of his writing?
- What interests have you pursued as writing topics, and why?

_____

_____

_____

_____

Segment 2: James Berry Introduces "Lucy: Englan' Lady"
- What inspired James Berry to write the poem "Lucy: Englan' Lady"?
- How does James Berry's reading of this poem change the way you might understand it if you read the poem yourself?

_____

_____

_____

_____

Segment 3: The Writing Process
- What process does James Berry follow when he develops a character?
- As a writer, do you think you would rather create characters from your own imagination or base them on real people? Explain your answer.

_____

_____

_____

_____

Segment 4: The Rewards of Writing
- James Berry believes that literature helps "widen the human vision of experience." What do you think he means by this?
- What do you think you can learn about yourself by reading and writing?

_____

_____

_____

_____

Vocabulary Warm-up Word Lists

Study these words from the selections. Then, complete the activities.

Word List A

vast [VAST] *adj.* very large; great in size
  The United States is a <u>vast</u> country.

widow [WID oh] *n.* woman whose husband has died
  The <u>widow</u> had many happy memories of her departed husband.

tide [TYD] *n.* the rise and fall of ocean waters each day
  The high <u>tide</u> washed away items left on the beach.

ebb [EB] *n.* lessening or decline
  She felt an <u>ebb</u> in her pain after taking her medicine.

fling [FLING] *v.* throw with great force
  Don't <u>fling</u> your litter out the car window.

valiant [VAL yuhnt] *adj.* brave
  The <u>valiant</u> hero saved many people during the hurricane.

furled [FERLD] *adj.* rolled up tightly
  The awning on the storefront was <u>furled</u> during the storm to keep it from flapping.

retreating [ri TREET ing] *v.* going back or going away
  When the rain stopped, the flood waters began <u>retreating</u> into the river.

Word List B

tremulous [TREM yoo luhs] *adj.* trembling; shaking
  The leaves were <u>tremulous</u> during the big storm.

blanched [BLANCHT] *adj.* pale; whitened
  After the accident, her face looked <u>blanched</u>.

certitude [SERT uh tood] *n.* sureness
  He answered our questions with confidence and <u>certitude</u>.

lest [LEST] *conj.* for fear that
  Check your packing list twice <u>lest</u> you forget something important.

tumult [TOO muhlt] *n.* noise and confusion
  There was great <u>tumult</u> in the stadium after the championship game.

glimmering [GLIM er ing] *adj.* giving a faint, flickering light
  We saw tiny fish <u>glimmering</u> as they swam through the pond.

grating [GRAYT ing] *adj.* making a harsh, grinding sound
  The <u>grating</u> sound of the car's motor told us it needed repairs.

frantic [FRANT ik] *adj.* wild with anger or worry
  My parents were <u>frantic</u> when I came home two hours late.

"Dover Beach" by Matthew Arnold
"Recessional" and **"The Widow at Windsor"** by Rudyard Kipling
Vocabulary Warm-up Exercises

Exercise A *Fill in each blank in the paragraph below using each word from Word List A only once.*

As the [1] _____ walked along the beach, she looked out into the distance

at the [2] _____ ocean, which extended as far as the eye could see. In

her hand, she carried an umbrella, [3] _____ for now, but easy to open in

case a storm blew in. Lost in thought, she watched the ocean [4] _____

come in, and she heard it [5] _____ pebbles and shells onto the shore.

As she watched, she remembered her [6] _____ husband, who had lived

and died so bravely. Then, observing the [7] _____ of the weakening

waves, she brought her thoughts back to the present. As her memories were

[8] _____, she was appreciating the beauty of the land and sea around her.

Exercise B *Decide whether each of the following statements is true or false. Circle T or F, and explain your answers.*

1. The sound of a chain rubbing against a metal bar would be <u>grating</u>.
   T / F _____

2. You should wear a bicycle helmet <u>lest</u> you fall and hit your head.
   T / F _____

3. A calm person is likely to be <u>tremulous</u>.
   T / F _____

4. Bright summer sunshine at noon could be described as <u>glimmering</u>.
   T / F _____

5. A person running late through an airport to board a plane might be <u>frantic</u>.
   T / F _____

6. Someone about to faint might look <u>blanched</u>.
   T / F _____

7. To feel <u>certitude</u> about making the right decision is a good feeling.
   T / F _____

8. A peaceful summer lake at sunset is a scene of great <u>tumult</u>.
   T / F _____

Name _____ Date _____

"Dover Beach" by Matthew Arnold
"Recessional" and **"The Widow at Windsor"** by Rudyard Kipling
Reading Warm-up A

Read the following passage. Pay special attention to the underlined words. Then, read it again, and complete the activities. Use a separate sheet of paper for your written answers.

In the 1800s, many fishing families lived on the northeast coast of England. The men set off into the <u>vast</u> Atlantic, often sailing for several days across the great ocean to search for good fishing spots. If a storm came up, the fishermen rode it out. They had the sails of their boats tightly <u>furled</u> to keep them from blowing away. Mighty winds would <u>fling</u> the boats across the water as an angry child would throw a toy.

These people knew the sea was dangerous. Many a <u>widow</u> mourned a husband who had died on the job. To help save lives, communities formed rescue squads, <u>valiant</u> friends and neighbors who were brave enough to oppose the stormy sea. Usually, it was the women who launched the rescue boats. They waded into the water and dragged the boats out against the powerful incoming <u>tide</u>. The tide was often strong enough to knock them down and turn over the lifeboats.

People of the coast even rescued the passengers of steamships. One famous rescuer was Grace Darling, the daughter of a lighthouse keeper on Farne Island. When the steamship *Forfarshire* sank near the island, Grace's father rescued nine survivors. The survivors were clinging to rocks near the shore. Instead of <u>retreating</u> to safety further inland, Grace insisted on helping her father. Thanks to their efforts, all nine passengers were brought to safety in the lighthouse.

With the <u>ebb</u> of the ocean waters after the storm had passed, the grateful survivors were able to make their journeys home. They spread the story of Grace Darling, and Grace became the hero of many poems and songs.

1. Underline the words that give a hint to the meaning of the word <u>vast</u>. Give a synonym for **vast**.

2. Underline the words that suggest the meaning of the word <u>furled</u>. Tell what **furled** means.

3. Underline the comparison that helps you understand the meaning of <u>fling</u>. Use **fling** in a sentence.

4. Underline the words that hint at the meaning of <u>widow</u>. Tell what **widow** means.

5. Circle the word that is a synonym for <u>valiant</u>. Give an antonym for **valiant**.

6. Underline the words that hint at the meaning of the word <u>tide</u>. Tell what **tide** means.

7. Underline words that suggest the meaning of the word <u>retreating</u>. Use **retreating** in a sentence.

8. Underline the words that hint at the meaning of the word <u>ebb</u>. Tell what **ebb** means.

"**Dover Beach**" by Matthew Arnold
"**Recessional**" and "**The Widow at Windsor**" by Rudyard Kipling
Reading Warm-up B

Read the following passage. Pay special attention to the underlined words. Then, read it again, and complete the activities. Use a separate sheet of paper for your written answers.

As the British Empire grew, many English citizens settled in faraway colonies, such as India. In the early 1800s, there were no passenger ships that made the long journey to India. Instead, travelers depended on the cargo ships of the East India Company to transport them. Because of the dangers of shipwrecks, pirates, and attacks by enemy navies, these passengers had no <u>certitude</u> of reaching their destination alive.

An older passenger named William Hickey wrote a description of his 6-month-long journey from India back to England in 1808 on a ship called the *Castle Eden*. The ship's captain had advised Mr. Hickey not to take a room on the upper part of the ship, <u>lest</u> he be disturbed by the constant noise. Sailors worked directly above these rooms, creating a <u>tumult</u> of clanging, banging, and crashing activity all day long. Instead, Mr. Hickey took a room below decks. He instantly regretted his choice.

Ocean water leaked into his room. Instead of noisy sailors, it was the constant <u>grating</u> of moving metal parts in the ship's engine that kept him awake at night. His cabin was dark, and he had to read and write by the <u>glimmering</u> light of a single candle. After being tossed around his cabin by a storm that lasted for fourteen days, his face was <u>blanched</u> from seasickness and lack of sleep. His hands were so <u>tremulous</u> with fear that he could barely hold a cup of tea without spilling it. Mr. Hickey felt like a prisoner, rather than a passenger. He was <u>frantic</u> to escape his room. Luckily, the ship soon reached an island port where the passengers were able to rest on land for a week before continuing their long journey home.

1. Underline the examples of things that kept passengers from having <u>certitude</u> of a safe journey. Tell what *certitude* means.

2. What words could you use to replace <u>lest</u> in this sentence so that the sentence would still make sense?

3. Circle the words that are clues to the meaning of <u>tumult</u>. Give a synonym for *tumult*.

4. Underline the phrase that describes the source of the <u>grating</u> sound. Describe something else that might make a *grating* sound.

5. Circle the word that identifies the source of the <u>glimmering</u> light. Give a synonym for *glimmering*.

6. Underline the words that describe the cause of Mr. Hickey's <u>blanched</u> face. Tell what *blanched* means.

7. Underline the words that describe the cause and effect of Mr. Hickey's <u>tremulous</u> hands. Use the word *tremulous* in a sentence.

8. Underline the comparison that gives a hint to the meaning of the word <u>frantic</u>. Give a synonym for *frantic*.

"Dover Beach" by Matthew Arnold
"Recessional" and **"The Widow at Windsor"** by Rudyard Kipling
Literary Analysis: Mood as a Key to Theme

The feelings that a poem creates in the reader make up the **mood** of the poem. How you feel after you read a poem can give you a hint as to the poem's central idea, or **theme.**

If you finish reading a poem feeling happy, the poem likely expressed an optimistic outlook or a pleasing image. If, however, a poem's theme has to do with the evils of imperialism, for example, it probably will not contain optimism or pleasing images. A reader might come away from such a poem feeling threatened, sober, or scared. Those feelings can be a clue that the poem's central idea is to be taken seriously.

To create mood, poets use vivid images and words that have emotional appeal. Notice how Matthew Arnold creates a rhythm that imitates the sound of the ocean. Notice, too, the vivid verbs and adjectives he uses, which have more emotional appeal than less colorful language.

> Listen! you hear the grating roar
> Of pebbles which the waves draw back, and fling,
> At their return, up the high strand,
> Begin, and cease, and then again begin,
> With tremulous cadence slow, and bring
> The eternal note of sadness in.

DIRECTIONS: *Following each passage, describe the mood of the passage—the feelings the passage creates in you—and indicate the words or phrases that create that mood. Then, interpret those feelings in connection with the theme of that poem.*

1. lines 9–14 from "Dover Beach" (see above)

   _____
   _____
   _____
   _____

2. lines 13–18 from "Recessional":

   > Far-called, our navies melt away—
   > On dune and headland sinks the fire—
   > Lo, all our pomp of yesterday
   > Is one with Nineveh and Tyre!
   > Judge of the Nations, spare us yet,
   > Lest we forget—lest we forget!

   _____
   _____
   _____
   _____

"Dover Beach" by Matthew Arnold
"Recessional" and **"The Widow at Windsor"** by Rudyard Kipling
Reading Strategy: Relate Mood and Theme to Historical Period

The Victorian Era in England was marked by change. Progress in science led to the questioning of religious faith. There was a huge disparity between rich and poor. The expansion of the British Empire brought much anxiety and tension. All of these factors are present in the **mood and theme** of literature written during this **historical period.** A reader can better understand the poems in this section by keeping the historical context in mind while reading the poems.

DIRECTIONS: *Use the chart below to record lines of poetry that show how different aspects of the historical period relate to the mood and theme of each poem. If you do not find a relationship between a poem and an aspect of the historical period, you may leave a box blank.*

	Questioning of Religious Faith	Disparity of the Classes	Tensions of War and Expansion
"Dover Beach"	1.	2.	3.
"Recessional"	4.	5.	6.
"The Widow at Windsor"	7.	8.	9.

"Dover Beach" by Matthew Arnold
"Recessional" and **"The Widow at Windsor"** by Rudyard Kipling
Vocabulary Builder

Using the Root -domi-

A. DIRECTIONS: *From the Latin* dominus, *English acquires several words whose meanings relate to the word's meaning of "lord" or "master." Keep this in mind as you answer questions about some words that include the -domi- root. Use a dictionary if you wish.*

1. How is someone who *dominates* different from someone who *domineers*?

_____

2. Portuguese and Brazilian royalty are allowed to add the word *Dom* to their names, as a sign of their status. What, in your opinion, does this signify?

_____

3. What is an *indomitable* enemy?

_____

Using the Word List

awe   cadence   contrite   dominion   tranquil   turbid

B. DIRECTIONS: *Match each word in the left column with its definition in the right column. Write the letter of the definition on the line next to the word it defines.*

___ 1. cadence   A. repenting for sin
___ 2. contrite   B. murky
___ 3. dominion   C. reverence, fear, and wonder
___ 4. tranquil   D. free from disturbance
___ 5. turbid   E. rhythmic sequence
___ 6. awe   F. power

"Dover Beach" by Matthew Arnold
"Recessional" and **"The Widow at Windsor"** by Rudyard Kipling
Integrated Language Skills: Support for Writing

Use the charts below to gather details for your response to critic Walter E. Houghton's statement that the Victorian Age was characterized by "widespread doubt about the nature of man, society, and the universe." Then, use your information to write a thesis statement for your essay.

"Recessional"

	Images	Moods	Themes
Doubt			
Self-Confidence			

"The Widow at Windsor"

	Images	Moods	Themes
Doubt			
Self-Confidence			

Thesis Statement (agree or disagree with Houghton's statement):

_____

_____

_____

On a separate page, use the thesis statement to help you write your response. Support your thesis with the details you have gathered from the poems.

"Dover Beach" by Matthew Arnold
"Recessional" and **"The Widow at Windsor"** by Rudyard Kipling
Enrichment: Science

The limestone and chalk of what is now England's southern coastline has been and continues to be worn away by the constant action of the Atlantic Ocean and the North Sea. The waves that lap at or pound on any coastline change that coastline constantly in three ways:

- The face of a cliff has tiny cracks and crevices. As a wave splashes into a crack, the air in the crack is compressed. The air has to go somewhere, so it gets driven into the rock. When the wave falls away, the pressure is suddenly released. This **hydraulic action**—continual changes in air pressure—weakens the cliff face, causing pieces to break off.
- Waves carry sand and pebbles as they break against a cliff. This constant **corrosive action** at the base of the cliff wears out a notch. The cliff face above weakens and eventually collapses.
- The water of the ocean is slightly acidic. Acidic water easily dissolves rocks that contain chalk or limestone. Wherever the waves contact these rocks, their **solvent action** goes to work.

The shape of a coastline, the makeup of its rocks, and the local tides and currents all affect how quickly a coastline changes. In separate studies of land loss in England, geologists studied two separate points along the coast. Both areas present cliff faces to the cold North Sea. At Point A, land loss was 9 feet per year; Point B lost 6.5 feet per year. This bar graph illustrates the cumulative loss of land in those locations.

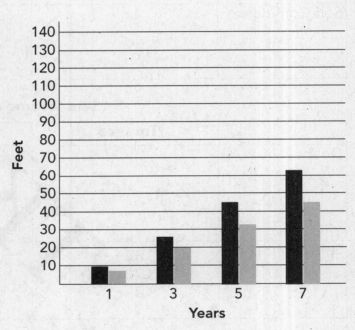

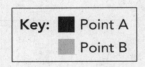

Key: ■ Point A　■ Point B

DIRECTIONS: *Use the text and the bar graph on this page to answer the questions that follow.*

1. Calculate the cumulative land loss for Years 9, 11, 13, and 15. Extend the *x*-axis on the graph on this page and add labels. Graph the results of your calculations.

2. There is much debate about whether we should try to control coastline erosion or let land and water find their own balance. Sea walls, jetties, and other methods are costly and vary in effectiveness. What might be the pros and cons of trying to stop or slow the ocean's effects on the world's coastlines?

_____

_____

_____

Name _____ Date _____

Poems by Matthew Arnold and Rudyard Kipling
Open-Book Test

Short Answer *Write your responses to the questions in this section on the lines provided.*

1. From Matthew Arnold's description of the sea in the first stanza of "Dover Beach," what inference can you make about the speaker's mood at this point in the poem? Explain your answer by using specific references from the poem.

   _____

   _____

   _____

   _____

2. Reread the first three stanzas of "Dover Beach" (lines 1–20). How does the speaker perceive the sea, and how does his perception relate to the history of humankind?

   _____

   _____

   _____

   _____

3. What sad conclusion does the speaker reach in the last stanza of "Dover Beach"? How may this conclusion relate to the historical period in which the poem was written?

   _____

   _____

   _____

   _____

4. In "Recessional," Rudyard Kipling directs his words to a particular listener, but his message is designed for a larger audience. Whom does the speaker specifically address, and who represents the broader audience?

   _____

   _____

   _____

   _____

5. Which word would you choose to describe the mood of "Recessional"? Briefly explain how this mood relates to the poem's central theme.

   _____

   _____

   _____

   _____

6. As reflected in "Recessional," how does Kipling seem to feel about the British Empire? Use quotations or examples from the poem to explain your answer.

_____

_____

_____

7. Who is the "Widow at Windsor" referred to in the title of Kipling's poem? Explain how you know who she is.

_____

_____

_____

8. "The Widow at Windsor" is written so that the reader understands the speaker's cockney accent. Give two examples of this dialect, and then explain why Kipling might have chosen to write the poem in dialect.

_____

_____

_____

9. If you are in a *tranquil* mood, do you feel peaceful or troubled?

_____

_____

_____

10. Use a graphic organizer like the one shown below to gather details about the mood of "The Widow at Windsor." Then, analyze the mood to determine the theme of the poem. Write a statement of the theme in the space provided in the organizer.

Mood Detail	**Mood Detail**	**Mood Detail**

Theme

Essay

Write an extended response to the question of your choice or to the question or questions your teacher assigns you.

11. Write an essay in which you explore the mood of Matthew Arnold's "Dover Beach." Include examples from the poem and conclude by stating the theme of the poem.

12. In an essay, describe the sea that the speaker of Arnold's "Dover Beach" is observing, and also the "Sea of Faith" to which the literal sea is compared. As you write, draw conclusions about the connections between the details in the description of each "sea."

13. In an essay, compare and contrast Arnold's and Kipling's attitudes toward the British Empire, as indicated by these poems: "Dover Beach," "Recessional," and "The Widow at Windsor." Support your main ideas with specific references to the selections.

14. **Thinking About the Essential Question: Does a sense of place shape literature, or does literature shape a sense of place?** In an essay, discuss how the specific places referred to in Matthew Arnold's "Dover Beach" and Rudyard Kipling's "The Widow at Windsor" help ground both poems in a setting that influences the mood, tone, and theme of the works. Be sure to support your main ideas with specific references to the selections.

Oral Response

15. Go back to question 1, 2, 3, 6, 8, 10, or the question your teacher assigns you. Take a few minutes to expand your answer and to prepare an oral response. Find additional details in the selections that support your points. If necessary, make an outline to guide your oral response.

"Dover Beach" by Matthew Arnold
"Recessional" and **"The Widow at Windsor"** by Rudyard Kipling
Selection Test A

Critical Reading *Identify the letter of the choice that best answers the question.*

____ 1. The speaker is comparing what two things in "Dover Beach"?
    A. the beach and darkness
    B. the ocean and the beach
    C. the tides and human life
    D. the sea and war

____ 2. Which line from "Dover Beach" best expresses the mood of the poem?
    A. "Listen! you hear the grating roar / Of pebbles . . ."
    B. "Sophocles long ago / Heard it on the Aegean . . ."
    C. "Find also in the sound a thought, / Hearing it by this distant northern sea."
    D. "But now I only hear / Its melancholy, long, withdrawing roar. . . ."

____ 3. What Victorian attitude toward religious faith is reflected in the poem "Dover Beach"?
    A. Traditional religious faith was coming into question.
    B. Traditional religious faith was growing stronger.
    C. Religious faith had become more powerful, like the tides.
    D. People were looking for religious faith in the wrong places.

____ 4. What is the speaker's view of the world in "Dover Beach"?
    A. The world is a calm, forgiving, and beautiful home.
    B. The world is a place of sadness, misery, and violence.
    C. The world is a place of peace and calm for those who seek it.
    D. The world is always changing and people should accept it.

____ 5. Who is the speaker addressing in "Recessional"?
    A. the English people
    B. Queen Victoria
    C. the people of the world
    D. God

____ 6. What is the main idea of Kipling's "Recessional"?
    A. The British empire will not last forever.
    B. The British empire is the most powerful nation in history.
    C. The British empire will always be remembered.
    D. The British empire has made the world a safer place.

____ 7. What does the speaker mean in these lines from "Recessional"?
    For heathen heart that puts her trust/In reeking tube and iron shard—
    All valiant dust that builds on dust,/And guarding calls not Thee to guard . . .

    A. The English people believe their armies cannot protect them.
    B. People think they can maintain their empire only through war.
    C. People put their faith in their armies and do not ask God to protect them.
    D. The English people are uneducated and know only how to wage war.

____ 8. Who is the widow in "The Widow at Windsor"?
   A. the speaker's mother
   B. the poet's mother
   C. the British flag
   D. Queen Victoria

____ 9. In "The Widow at Windsor," what can you tell about the speaker's place in society from the dialect?
   A. He is a member of the royal family.
   B. He is a world-famous poet.
   C. He is a common person.
   D. He is well educated.

____ 10. What is the theme of "The Widow at Windsor"?
   A. Most British rulers care about the well-being of their people.
   B. The queen's greatness was paid for with the lives of English soldiers.
   C. Great rulers achieved greatness through courage and self-sacrifice.
   D. Britain owes its greatness to the wisdom and power of the queen.

____ 11. What conclusion about the historical period of the poem can you draw from these lines from "The Widow at Windsor"?

   We 'ave 'eard o' the Widow at Windsor,
   It's safest to leave 'er alone:
   For 'er sentries we stand by the sea an' the land
   Wherever the bugles are blown.

   A. The speaker is a farmer.
   B. The speaker is in the queen's military.
   C. The queen never forgives her enemies.
   D. The queen wants to keep England out of war.

Vocabulary and Grammar

____ 12. Which is the best synonym for the word *dominion* in this line from "Recessional"?
   Beneath whose awful Hand we hold
   Dominion over palm and pine. . . .

   A. control
   B. arms
   C. peace
   D. location

____ 13. Which sentence **incorrectly** uses a vocabulary word?
   A. In the poem "Dover Beach," the cliffs look out over a *tranquil* sea.
   B. The *turbid* waters of the pounding tides threw sand high up on the beach.
   C. The melancholy scene brought a chill *cadence* to the back of my neck.
   D. Few English people felt at all *contrite* over the great power of Britain.

____ **14.** Which line from Arnold's "Dover Beach" is in a tense other than the present tense?
   A. "The sea is calm tonight."
   B. " . . . on the French coast the light / Gleams and is gone. . . ."
   C. "Ah, love, let us be true / To one another!"
   D. "Sophocles long ago / Heard it on the Aegean . . ."

Essay

15. The speaker talks about several subjects in "Dover Beach": the beach and tide, the "Sea of Faith," and love. Write an essay in which you identify and explain the message of this poem. Explain how the different subjects contribute to the message. Use details from the poem to support your response.

16. Do you think Kipling was proud of his country's power and achievements? In an essay, explain how the poems "Recessional" and "The Widow at Windsor" demonstrate his personal feelings toward the British empire. Use details from the poem to support your explanation.

17. **Thinking About the Essential Question: Does sense of place shape literature, or does literature shape sense of place?** In an essay, discuss the specific places referred to in Matthew Arnold's "Dover Beach" and Rudyard Kipling's "The Widow at Windsor." Where does each poem take place? What details about place does each poem provide? Next, connect the setting to the mood, tone, and theme of each poem to the place. How does the place create a mood and tone for the reader? How does the place relate to the theme of the poem? Be sure to support your main ideas with specific references to the selections.

"Dover Beach" by Matthew Arnold
"Recessional" and **"The Widow at Windsor"** by Rudyard Kipling
Selection Test B

Critical Reading *Identify the letter of the choice that best completes the statement or answers the question.*

_____ 1. What view of the world does the speaker of "Dover Beach" express?
   A. The world is a calm place, much like the feeling one has when watching ocean waves roll in.
   B. The world is only a struggle of constant violence.
   C. The world does not contain joy or love or peace for those who dwell in it.
   D. The world is and always has been a place of sadness, with no hope of any change.

_____ 2. From the details in "Dover Beach," what conclusion can you draw about the Victorian people's attitude about religion?
   A. Victorians had a strong faith that was unshakable.
   B. Victorians always went to church to pray.
   C. Victorians were opposed to poetry that lacked religious themes.
   D. People were questioning religion.

_____ 3. What emotional words does Arnold use in the passage about the "Sea of Faith" to create mood?
   A. Sea of Faith, full, night
   B. melancholy, withdrawing, retreating
   C. earth's shore, night wind, naked shingles
   D. Lay, hear, down

_____ 4. How do the sensory images in the first two stanzas of "Dover Beach" create mood?
   A. The waves smashing against the cliffs create an angry, violent mood.
   B. The unseen reaches of the sea at night create an ominous mood.
   C. The rhythmic flow of the ocean's waves creates a peaceful mood.
   D. The moonlight and the isolation of the beach create a mysterious mood.

_____ 5. To whom is "Recessional" addressed?
   A. to Queen Victoria
   B. to the British Empire
   C. to the poet
   D. to God

_____ 6. What do Kipling's words "we hold / Dominion over palm and pine—" refer to?
   A. human control over nature
   B. the variety of God's creation
   C. the extent of the British Empire
   D. the speaker's view as he addresses the poem's subject

____ 7. How do the last two lines of this passage affect the mood of the stanza?

> God of our fathers, known of old— / Lord of our far-flung battle-line— / Beneath whose awful Hand we hold / Dominion over palm and pine— / Lord God of Hosts, be with us yet / Lest we forget—lest we forget!

A. They create a sense of sincere desperation.
B. They create an old-fashioned feeling with the use of the word *lest*.
C. They reveal the speaker's sense of abandonment, creating an angry mood.
D. They create a prayer-like mood that brings out religious feelings in the reader.

____ 8. What conclusion about the poet's historical period can you draw from these lines?

> Lo, all our pomp of yesterday / Is one with Nineveh and Tyre!

A. The speaker feels Britain's greatness is similar to that of ancient cities.
B. The speaker believes the greatness of Britain could disappear, just as did that of Nineveh and Tyre.
C. The speaker feels that the greatness of Britain will be everlasting, like that of Nineveh and Tyre.
D. The speaker believes that great cities or nations all hold the same attitudes toward power and success, which contribute to their greatness.

____ 9. To whom does the title of "The Widow at Windsor" refer?
A. the speaker's mother
B. the poet's mother
C. an old woman in an old house
D. Queen Victoria

____ 10. What conclusion can you draw about the speaker and his place in society from this passage?

> Walk wide o' the Widow at Windsor,
>   For 'alf o' Creation she owns: We 'ave bought 'er
> the same with the sword an' the flame,
>   An' we've salted it down with our bones.

A. The speaker is an enemy of the Widow and wishes to avoid her.
B. The speaker is a warrior who uses sword and flame to get what he wants.
C. The speaker is a soldier who serves in the Widow's army.
D. The speaker against material wealth views the Widow as a ruthless materialist who owns everything she can get her hands on.

____ 11. Which aspect of "The Widow at Windsor" reveals the common nature of the speaker?
A. the dialect
B. the use of the sentences in parentheses
C. the attitude expressed about the Widow
D. the use of the phrase "Widow at Windsor"

____ 12. The informal, slightly disrespectful mood of "The Widow at Windsor" helps lead readers to the poem's theme, which is that
   A. soldiers always rebel against their leaders.
   B. rulers always think of their soldiers as inferior, or "underlings."
   C. rulers are far removed from the realities of empire building.
   D. the Empire is great, but greatness comes with a price.

Vocabulary and Grammar

On the line, write the letter of the one best answer.

____ 13. Arnold describes an ocean bay that is *tranquil,* or
   A. calm and smooth.
   B. frothy with white-capped waves.
   C. deep and dark.
   D. a very pleasant place.

____ 14. Kipling's poems both have to do with *dominion,* which means
   A. a kind of residence.
   B. a type of influence.
   C. a place of rule.
   D. a kind of service.

____ 15. Choose the sentence that contains a present-tense verb.
   A. The cliffs of England stand, glimmering and vast, out in the Straits of Dover.
   B. Sophocles heard it long ago on the Aegean Sea.
   C. The Sea of Faith was once, too, at the full and lay around the shore.
   D. The world would have no comfort for those who sought it.

____ 16. Which are functions of present-tense verbs?
   A. expressing actions recently completed and to be completed
   B. expressing current action and general truths
   C. expressing intended action and characters' actions in a story or poem
   D. expressing past action and ongoing consequences

Essay

17. Kipling wrote "Recessional" more than a hundred years ago at the height of England's power. What is the message of the poem, and what does it say about power and people? Write an essay in which you explain how Kipling's commentary on vanished ancient cities applies to us today. Use examples from the poem to illustrate your points.

18. Kipling was considered an imperialist. That means he favored the influence and power that Great Britain held over far-flung corners of the world. In an essay, discuss whether Kipling's belief in imperialism emerges in these poems. Cite passages that lead to your conclusion.

19. **Thinking About the Essential Question: Does sense of place shape literature, or does literature shape sense of place?** In an essay, discuss how the specific places referred to in Matthew Arnold's "Dover Beach" and Rudyard Kipling's "The Widow at Windsor" help ground both poems in a setting that influences the mood, tone, and theme of the works. Be sure to support your main ideas with specific references to the selections.

Primary Sources: "Progress in Personal Comfort" and Cook's Railroad Advertisement
Primary Sources Worksheet

Advertisements always use persuasion in order to convince consumers to purchase a product and/or service. An article in a newspaper may or may not use persuasion depending on the topic and the author's purpose. Articles in which an author shares his or her opinion are often intended to convince the reader that the writer's point of view is correct.

The four modes of persuasion are:

1. logical: presents factual evidence and arguments that make sense
2. faulty: presents arguments that do not make sense
3. deceptive: presents intentionally misleading information
4. emotional: uses status symbols, peer pressure, patriotism, humor, or appeals to reader's emotions

DIRECTIONS: *Use the table below to identify and compare the means of persuasion used in the primary source selections. Some boxes may be blank.*

	Progress in Personal Comfort	Cook's Railroad Advertisement
1. Logical		
2. Faulty		
3. Deceptive		
4. Emotional		

5. What differences do you notice in persuasion techniques used in each primary source?

_____

_____

_____

Primary Sources: "Progress in Personal Comfort" and Cook's Railroad Advertisement
Vocabulary Builder

Using the Word List

bilious	depredation	fracture	gout
macadam	privations	pulp	

A. DIRECTIONS: *On the line, write the Word List word that best completes each sentence.*

1. The man fell on the dark streets, causing a _____ in his knee.

2. _____ was an untreatable disease before the invention of calomel.

3. Streets in Victorian England were often made of _____.

4. Smith lists the _____ of his life when he was young.

5. Cook's trip would not be enjoyable if a traveler was _____.

6. Smith's hat was reduced to a _____ in the rain.

7. Smith describes the old times as dangerous because of the _____.

B. DIRECTIONS: *Match each word in the left column with its definition in the right column. Write the letter of the definition on the line next to the word it defines.*

___ 1. depredation		A.	losses
___ 2. macadam		B.	having a digestive ailment
___ 3. fracture		C.	soft, formless mass
___ 4. pulp		D.	type of arthritis
___ 5. gout		E.	broken bone
___ 6. bilious		F.	road surfacing
___ 7. privations		G.	robbing

Selection Test: Informational Texts

"Progress in Personal Comfort" and Cook's Railroad Advertisement

Critical Reading *Identify the letter of the choice that best answers the question.*

____ 1. What is the author's purpose in writing the newspaper article, "Progress in Personal Comfort?
   A. to advertise some new inventions
   B. to inform about new inventions that are available to consumers
   C. to persuade readers that times have changed for the better in terms of comfort and safety
   D. to persuade people to live in London

____ 2. What kind of persuasive technique is used in the following passage from "Progress in Personal Comfort?"
   > It took me nine hours to go from Taunton to Bath' before the invention of railroads, and I now go in six hours from Taunton to London!
   A. faulty
   B. logical
   C. emotional
   D. deceptive

____ 3. What kind of persuasive technique is used in the following passage from "Progress in Personal Comfort?"
   > There were no waterproof hats, and *my* hat has often been reduced by rains into its primitive pulp.
   A. faulty
   B. logical
   C. emotional
   D. deceptive

____ 4. Which is not an example of progress that Smith cites?
   A. gas street lamps
   B. faster travel
   C. safer streets
   D. airplanes

____ 5. What are the primary techniques that are used in the Cook's Railroad advertisement?
   A. faulty and logical
   B. faulty and emotional
   C. emotional and deceptive
   D. logical and deceptive

____ 6. Which of the two primary sources, "Progress in Personal Comfort" and the Cook's Railroad advertisement, would have reached? readers who were educated and affluent?

    A. both

    B. neither

    C. "Progress in Personal Comfort" only

    D. Cooks Railroad ad only

____ 7. Smith's article implies that

    A. more modern comforts are anticipated by society.

    B. many people did not appreciate the comforts that technology brought.

    C. people in his time hated the railroad and the police.

    D. people wanted more changes and wanted them quickly.

____ 8. What is the purpose of the Cook's Railroad advertisement?

    A. to inform about the railroad

    B. to persuade that the railroad is superior to air travel

    C. to persuade people to take rail trips

    D. to entertain with humor

Essay

9. Write a news article that persuades people that a certain modern-day technology has been beneficial to society. Choose a technology that is somewhat controversial, and address people's concerns about that technology.

Vocabulary Warm-up Word Lists

Study these words from the selections. Then, complete the activities.

Word List A

pulse [PUHLS] *n.* regular or rhythmical beating; throb
   The pulse of the music was created by the drumbeat.

check [CHEK] *v.* arrest the motion of; halt; restrain
   You can check the flow of water in that pipe by shutting the valve.

shone [SHOHN] *v.* emitted light; glowed
   Happiness shone in her eyes when she found her lost dog.

canopy [KAN uh pee] *n.* a high overarching covering, such as the sky or trees
   The canopy in the forest prevents most sunlight from reaching the ground.

dreary [DRIR ee] *adj.* dismal; boring; gloomy; dull
   The weather has been dreary this week with constant rain and gray skies.

bleak [BLEEK] *adj.* depressing; providing no encouragement
   After months without work, the actor felt his prospects were bleak.

sternly [STURN lee] *adv.* harshly; severely; firmly
   The teacher spoke to the class sternly, warning them not to misbehave.

existence [ig ZIS tens] *n.* the state of continued being; life
   The existence of many plants and animals is threatened by pollution.

Word List B

cherished [CHER ishd] *v.* held dear; treated with tenderness; appreciated
   The elderly woman cherished her photo album.

ecstatic [ek STAT ik] *adj.* being in a state of ecstasy; joyful; enraptured
   When the man learned he had won the lottery, he was ecstatic.

severed [SEV erd] *v.* divided or cut off
   After they divided the company, the former partners severed all business ties.

fidelity [fi DEL uh tee] *n.* faithfulness; loyalty
   The governor's campaign chairman was elected because of his fidelity to the party.

anguish [ANG gwish] *n.* agonizing physical or mental pain; torment
   Whenever I see a photo of a missing child, I think of the parents' anguish.

weaned [WEEND] *v.* to be detached from; ridden of dependence upon
   The man followed the doctor's orders and weaned himself from fatty foods.

frail [FRAYL] *adj.* weak and easily broken; delicate; fragile
   The kite was frail and came apart the first time it landed.

hasten [HAY sen] *v.* to speed up; to hurry
   She turned up the flame under the pot of soup to hasten the cooking time.

Name _____ Date _____

"Remembrance" by Emily Brontë
"The Darkling Thrush" and "Ah, Are You Digging on My Grave?" by Thomas Hardy
Vocabulary Warm-up Exercises

Exercise A *Fill in the blanks using each word from Word List A only once.*

Forests are natural wonders that [1] _____ with life and countless numbers of plants and animals. Despite the dark, [2] _____, and frightening reputation they earn in stories, forests provide everything needed to keep a human being alive when lost or stranded in the wilderness. Common sense and simple skills ensure someone's [3] _____. Conditions may look hopelessly [4] _____, but the [5] _____ of trees will provide initial shelter, and branches can be used to construct shelter that will protect the survivor from the elements. Often people lost in the woods were rescued when the light reflected from a mirror [6] _____ brightly enough to be spotted by a passing plane. To avoid becoming disoriented in thick brush, hikers should [7] _____ any impulse they have to wander off established trails. This warning is often repeated [8] _____, since too many have ignored it.

Exercise B *Answer each question with a complete sentence, replacing the underlined word with a word from Word List B that has a similar meaning.*

Example: Did the artist <u>hurry</u> to complete the portrait before the gallery opening?
    Sample answer: *Yes, the artist did <u>hasten</u> to complete the portrait before the opening.*

1. Was Grandma's wedding ring a <u>treasured</u> family heirloom?
   _____

2. Did Bill <u>break</u> contact with his neighbors when his family moved?
   _____

3. Will a dog behave with <u>loyalty</u> to its master?
   _____

4. Would winning a car make you feel <u>delighted</u>?
   _____

5. Has being sick ever made you feel <u>weak</u>?
   _____

6. Would you be in <u>misery</u> over a paper cut?
   _____

7. How old were you when you <u>deprived</u> yourself of your baby blanket?
   _____

"Remembrance" by Emily Brontë
"The Darkling Thrush" and "Ah, Are You Digging on My Grave?" by Thomas Hardy
Reading Warm-up A

Read the following passage. Pay special attention to the underlined words. Then, read it again, and complete the activities. Use a separate sheet of paper for your written answers.

As the digital face of Carrie's clock jumped to 5 A.M., her quiet apartment was filled with blaring noise. The alarm seemed louder than ever as it disrupted the gentle pulse of raindrops rhythmically hitting her window. Carrie rolled over in bed, reached for the "off" button, and with a practiced swipe, was able to check the incessant beeping. Even though it was still dark outside, she knew she would have regrets if she didn't stick to her schedule. So she got out of bed, drank some orange juice, and got ready for her morning jog.

As Carrie stepped out the door and into the dreary, rainy day, she had a smile on her face. A thick canopy of clouds and the slick, wet sidewalk gave the whole world a cold, gray appearance. She started along her usual route, dodging puddles, dog walkers, and other determined runners who were sternly refusing to let the bad weather interfere with their daily exercise. It was these days—the gray days—that Carrie loved best. The cold weather kept most people in their homes, making the park unusually quiet. This allowed the rhythm of her footsteps to be the only sound that broke the silence. This rainy atmosphere that others considered bleak and depressing, Carrie felt made her existence peaceful, and she was filled with tranquility as she jogged undisturbed through the empty park.

By the time she headed home, a weak sun shone through the clouds. While others greeted this with relief, Carrie felt she had already enjoyed the best part of the day.

1. Circle the words that describe the pulse of the raindrops. Then, explain what *pulse* means.

2. Circle the words that tell what Carrie wished to check. Then, describe something you'd like to *check*.

3. Rewrite the sentence using a synonym for dreary. Then, give an example of something you consider to be *dreary*.

4. Circle the words that tell what kind of canopy Carrie saw. Describe a different kind of *canopy*.

5. Rewrite the sentence using a synonym for sternly. Then, give an example of someone acting *sternly*.

6. Circle the words that tell what others thought was bleak. Name something you consider to be *bleak*.

7. Circle the words that show Carrie's existence was peaceful. Then, give a synonym for *existence*.

8. Rewrite the sentence using a synonym for shone. Then, describe something else that *shone*.

Name _____ Date _____

Read the following passage. Pay special attention to the underlined words. Then, read it again, and complete the activities. Use a separate sheet of paper for your written answers.

On his eleventh birthday, Michael finally received the gift he had been requesting since he was three years old: a golden retriever puppy. Naturally, he was <u>ecstatic</u>, and everyone in the family agreed they had never seen him so filled with joy. The dog was ten weeks old and had just been <u>weaned</u> from its mother, but there was nothing <u>frail</u> about this rambunctious, blond puppy; his belly was rotund and his paws were enormous.

In a matter of days, the dog, who was named Brian, had become a <u>cherished</u> and much-loved member of the clan. The pup responded to the love and attention that were showered on him with absolute loyalty and <u>fidelity</u>. Throughout the summer, he stayed by Michael's side, even bunking with him at night, an arrangement that suited him better than the basket and ticking clock that was supposed to re-create the sound of his mother's heartbeat.

Everyone anticipated the heartbreaking moment when this duo would be separated and there would be inevitable <u>anguish</u> for both the boy and his dog. They knew when school commenced this constant companionship would have to be <u>severed</u>. Although they spoke in hushed tones about the upcoming separation, they dreaded it— and certainly no one tried to <u>hasten</u> its impending arrival by keeping the boy and dog apart. Michael assured his parents that Brian would be calm when the time came to leave him because he had explained everything about his departure in detail, and the dog had understood what he was saying. His parents were skeptical and expected Brian to make a fuss when Michael left for school, but the dog behaved exactly as Michael had predicted: he waited patiently at the threshold until his young master returned home.

1. Circle the words that show Michael was <u>ecstatic</u>. Then, describe something that would make you *ecstatic*.

2. Circle the words that tell what the puppy had been <u>weaned</u> from. Then, describe something else that has to be *weaned*.

3. Underline the words that give clues about the opposite of <u>frail</u>. Then, give an example of something that is *frail*.

4. Circle the nearby word that is a synonym for <u>cherished</u>. Then, describe something you have *cherished*.

5. Underline the word that is a synonym for <u>fidelity</u>. Then, write a sentence telling how you might demonstrate *fidelity*.

6. Circle the word that means almost the same as <u>anguish</u>. Then, write a sentence using an antonym for *anguish*.

7. Circle the words that give clues to the meaning of <u>severed</u>. Then, give an example of something that was *severed*.

8. Underline the word that helps to explain what <u>hasten</u> means. Then, describe a time when someone tried to *hasten* you.

Name _____ Date _____

"Remembrance" by Emily Brontë
"The Darkling Thrush" and **"Ah, Are You Digging on My Grave?"**
by Thomas Hardy

Literary Analysis: Stanza Structure and Irony

A **stanza** usually contains a certain number of lines arranged to show a recurring pattern, rhythmic structure, and rhyme scheme. **Irony** is a deliberate contradiction between expectation and reality. Poets can establish certain expectations in their readers through a regular stanza structure. When poets then inject surprising events or ideas within the stanza structure, they create irony. The contrast between expectation and reality can make a poem more memorable.

DIRECTIONS: *Write your answers to the following questions on the chart.*

Questions for Analysis	"Remembrance"	"The Darkling Thrush"	"Ah, Are You Digging on My Grave?"
1. How many stanzas are in the poem?			
2. What is the stanza type (number of lines, meter, rhyme scheme)?			
3. What expectation is established by the stanza structure?			
4. What change or surprise occurs in the poem?			
5. What is the irony in the poem?			

"Remembrance" by Emily Brontë
"The Darkling Thrush" and **"Ah, Are You Digging on My Grave?"**
by Thomas Hardy

Reading Strategy: Reading Stanzas as Units of Meaning

Like paragraphs in prose, stanzas in poetry are usually a unit of meaning—they convey a main idea. Sometimes, a stanza will create a unified mood. Taken together, the stanzas of a poem express a larger theme or idea. As you read, analyze the stanzas in a poem for a progression of thoughts, a sequence of events, or a building of an argument or mood within the poem.

A. DIRECTIONS: *On the lines, write your answers to the following questions.*

1. In "Remembrance," what progression of thoughts or sequence of events does the speaker describe in stanzas one through five?

   _____

2. What change in the speaker's attitude occurs in stanzas six through eight?

   _____

3. What pattern is established in the first four stanzas of "Ah, Are You Digging on My Grave"?

   _____

B. DIRECTIONS: *On the flow chart, write a summary of each stanza in "The Darkling Thrush."*
Then write a sentence stating how the stanzas work together to create meaning.

Stanza 1:

↓

Stanza 2:

↓

Stanza 3:

↓

Stanza 4:

↓

Overall Meaning:

"Remembrance" by Emily Brontë
"The Darkling Thrush" and **"Ah, Are You Digging on My Grave?"** by Thomas Hardy
Vocabulary Builder

Using the Root -*terr(a)*-

A. DIRECTIONS: *Match each word in the left column with its definition in the right column. Write the letter of the definition on the line next to the word it defines.*

___ 1. territorial
___ 2. terrace
___ 3. subterranean
___ 4. terra-cotta
___ 5. terrarium

A. beneath the earth
B. fired clay used as building material
C. a glass container containing a garden of small plants and perhaps some small land animals
D. relating to a geographical area
E. a flat roof or paved outdoor space

Using the Word List

gaunt   languish   obscured   prodding   rapturous   terrestrial

B. DIRECTIONS: *On the line, write the Word List word that best completes the meaning of the sentence as a whole.*

1. The thrush in Hardy's poem sings a _____ song.
2. While in mourning, the woman refused to eat and became _____ and pale.
3. Who was _____ the dead woman's grave?
4. When a casket is buried, it is _____ by the soil above it.
5. The turn of the century causes the speaker to _____ rather than celebrate.
6. Unable to fly, the ostrich is a more _____ creature than other birds.

C. DIRECTIONS: *Fill in the blank with one of the vocabulary words to complete the analogies.*

1. _____ is to clear as night is to day
2. chubby is to _____ as tall is to short
3. happy is to _____ as sad is to miserable

"**Remembrance**" by Emily Brontë
"**The Darkling Thrush**" and "**Ah, Are You Digging on My Grave?**"
by Thomas Hardy

Grammar: Using Active Voice

When it is appropriate to the meaning of your sentence, use the active voice to lend vitality to your writing. The active voice can also help you cut down on unnecessary words. Consider the following example:

There was a deafening noise coming from the refrigerator.

A deafening noise came from the refrigerator.

DIRECTIONS: *Rewrite the following letter, using the active voice where appropriate.*

Dear Ms. Satchel,

   Your history class was enjoyed by me this semester. In fact, I think it was enjoyed by all of your students. Liveliness and a great atmosphere in the classroom were created by your sense of humor. Learning history has never been enjoyed by me until now. History was brought alive for me with your teaching. There is sadness in me because the year is ending.

   Your future students are envied by me to have you as a teacher. Hopefully, your summer will be great.

Your Student,

Nigel

"**Remembrance**" by Emily Brontë
"**The Darkling Thrush**" and "**Ah, Are You Digging on My Grave?**"
by Thomas Hardy
Integrated Language Skills: Support for Writing

Use the chart below to gather information for your comparison of literary sources. Use a variety of sources, such as an encyclopedia, an online review, or an article written by a scholar.

Title of work analyzed: _____

Source	Contents	Analysis

Choose two of the sources to draft your analysis. On a separate page, use details from the chart as you compare them to each other and analyze their literary value.

Name _____ Date _____

"Remembrance" by Emily Brontë
"The Darkling Thrush" and **"Ah, Are You Digging on My Grave?"**
by Thomas Hardy

Enrichment: Naturalism

As a Naturalist, Thomas Hardy was greatly affected by Charles Darwin's 1859 work *The Origin of Species.* Darwin's theories about biology, just one component of Naturalism, influenced Naturalists' view of individuals in society. Darwin theorized that every species evolves or develops from a previous one and that life is marked by continual change. In the process of evolution, species develop variations; those individuals who possess variations that enable them to adapt to their environment survive. They pass these adaptive variations on to their descendants. Individuals with variations not favored by the environment do not survive.

For Naturalists, this scientific theory had its corollary in social terms. Naturalists contended that individuals have little control over their own destinies. Instead, their lives are determined by their physical and social environment and often by pure chance. Many arbitrary and uncontrollable outside forces determine the condition of an individual's life.

DIRECTIONS: *The sentences in the left column are characteristics of Naturalism. The lettered items in the right column are lines from Hardy's poems. Match each characteristic in the left column with its representative lines in the right column. Write the letter of your choice in the blank.*

____ 1. Severe environmental conditions kill off individuals with unfavorable variations.

____ 2. Sentiment is of little use in the struggle for survival.

____ 3. The individual is of little importance in the environment.

____ 4. Impersonal forces determine individual actions, though those actions may be inappropriate.

A. "'. . . What good will planting flowers produce? / No tendance of her mound can loose / Her spirit from Death's gin.'"

B. "The ancient pulse of germ and birth / Was shrunken hard and dry."

C. "An aged thrush, frail, gaunt, and small, / In blast-beruffled plume, / Had chosen thus to fling his soul / Upon the growing gloom."

D. "Mistress, I dug upon your grave / To bury a bone . . . / . . . / I am sorry, but I quite forgot / It was your resting-place."

Poems by Emily Brontë and Thomas Hardy
Open-Book Test

Short Answer *Write your responses to the questions in this section on the lines provided.*

1. In the last line of Emily Brontë's poem "Remembrance," the speaker describes an empty world. What phrase would you use to identify this world? Explain your answer with reference to the speaker's situation.

   _____

   _____

   _____

2. In "Remembrance," what stanza structure does Emily Brontë use?

   _____

   _____

3. Describe at least two patterns that occur in the stanza structure of "Remembrance." Explain the effect of the patterns you describe.

   _____

   _____

   _____

4. In Thomas Hardy's poem "The Darkling Thrush," what is the speaker's perception of winter? Use examples of words or phrases from the poem to support your answer.

   _____

   _____

   _____

5. Identify the rhyming pattern in "The Darkling Thrush." How does this pattern contribute to the effect of the poem?

   _____

   _____

   _____

6. Briefly explain how "The Darkling Thrush" ends on an ironic note.

   _____

   _____

7. Who is the digger in Hardy's "'Ah, Are You Digging on My Grave?'"? Explain why the digger is at the grave.

   _____

   _____

   _____

8. Use the graphic organizer below to analyze the structure of "'Ah, Are You Digging on My Grave?'" In the boxes on the left, write short phrases that summarize the meaning of each of the poem's stanzas. Then, in the box on the right, identify how the poem's overall structure clearly produces the ironic effect at the end, when the last stanza shifts the tone that has been established in the previous five stanzas.

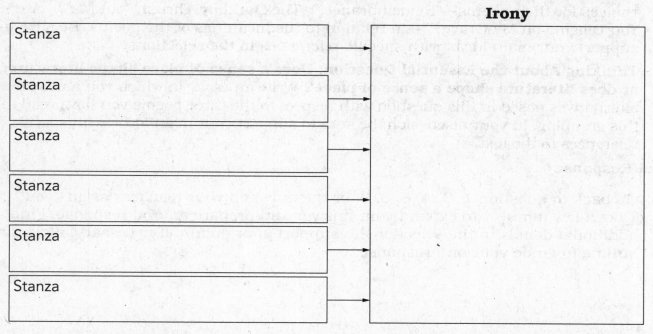

Irony

Stanza

Stanza

Stanza

Stanza

Stanza

Stanza

9. In "'Ah, Are You Digging on My Grave?'" why do you think the speaker questions who is digging on her grave?

_____

_____

_____

10. If you felt *rapturous,* would your mood be happy or sad?

_____

_____

_____

Essay

Write an extended response to the question of your choice or to the question or questions your teacher assigns you.

11. Emily Brontë and Thomas Hardy both use stanzas to present units of meaning, in the same way that paragraphs are used in prose. By linking the stanzas, these writers are able to develop the overall meaning of their poems. Brontë and Hardy are also alike in that they use the stanza structure to create irony in these poems. Choose one of the three poems, and write an essay in which you explain how the poet develops irony through the use of stanzas.

12. Consider the impressions you have from reading each of the poems by Brontë and Hardy. In an essay, analyze the effect of one of these poems, identifying what the poet wanted readers to feel or gain from the work. Use examples relating to the stanza structure and the outcome of the poem to support your points.

13. Write an essay in which you explain the significance of Brontë's and Hardy's title choices for their poems—"Remembrance," "The Darkling Thrush," and "'Ah, Are You Digging on My Grave?'"—in relation to the meanings of the poems. Be sure to support your main ideas with specific references to the selections.

14. **Thinking About the Essential Question: Does a sense of place shape literature, or does literature shape a sense of place?** Write an essay in which you assess the alternatives posed in this question with respect to the three poems you have read in this grouping. In your discussion, be sure to support your main ideas with specific references to the text.

Oral Response

15. Go back to question 1, 3, 4, 6, 8, 9, or the question your teacher assigns you. Take a few minutes to expand your answer and prepare an oral response. Find additional details in the selections to support your points. If necessary, make an outline to guide your oral response.

Name _____ Date _____

"Remembrance" by Emily Brontë
"The Darkling Thrush" and **"Ah, Are You Digging on My Grave?"** by Thomas Hardy
Selection Test A

Critical Reading *Identify the letter of the choice that best answers the question.*

____ 1. What does the speaker remember in "Remembrance"?
  A. her home
  B. her sister
  C. the one she loved
  D. her country

____ 2. What is the meaning of this stanza from "Remembrance"?
  Cold in the earth, and fifteen wild Decembers
  From these brown hills have melted into spring—
  Faithful indeed is the spirit that remembers
  After such years of change and suffering!

  A. It takes a special person to stay faithful to one who has been dead fifteen years.
  B. Fifteen cold years have passed and I still think of my beloved as if he were alive.
  C. It was cold when my beloved died, and it feels colder now when I remember him.
  D. I'll never forget the joys we had, which remind me of spring and the melting snow.

____ 3. What does the speaker in "Remembrance" plan to do?
  A. Forget her beloved.
  B. Live in mourning forever.
  C. Find a new love.
  D. Go on with her life.

____ 4. What is ironic about the song of the thrush in "The Darkling Thrush"?
  A. It is ironic that the speaker bothers to notice the thrush singing outside.
  B. It is ironic that only the thrush is singing when so many other birds are about.
  C. It is a winter day and nothing seems alive, but the thrush sings a cheerful song.
  D. The thrush is old and frail, and it is ironic that it can sing at all.

____ 5. How does the mood change from the beginning to the end of "The Darkling Thrush"?
  A. hopeless to hopeful
  B. hopeful to sad
  C. joyful to hopeless
  D. thoughtful to sad

____ 6. What is the main idea of "The Darkling Thrush"?
  A. None but birds would sing during the cold winter.
  B. Birds do not understand how sad life can be.
  C. Winter is the most difficult of seasons.
  D. Hope exists even during the worst of times.

_____ 7. Who is digging on the speaker's grave in "Ah, Are You Digging on My Grave?"
   A. the speaker's beloved
   B. the speaker's family
   C. the speaker's dog
   D. the speaker's enemy

_____ 8. What is the main idea of "Ah, Are You Digging on My Grave?"
   A. We are forgotten after we die.
   B. People who loved us will remember us always.
   C. No one escapes death, not even poets.
   D. Only pets remember us after death.

_____ 9. What do you learn about the poem "Ah, Are You Digging on My Grave?" by connecting the ideas expressed in each stanza?
   A. The speaker is dead.
   B. The death of the speaker was sudden.
   C. Life is a sad and lonely existence.
   D. The poem is deeply sentimental.

_____ 10. What is the main irony of "Ah, Are You Digging on My Grave?"
   A. The speaker asks many questions.
   B. Pets usually remember their owners.
   C. Her beloved has forgotten her after her death.
   D. The speaker expects someone to grieve for her.

Vocabulary and Grammar

_____ 11. Which vocabulary word best describes the thrush in "The Darkling Thrush"?
   A. languish
   B. unaware
   C. gaunt
   D. terrestrial

_____ 12. Which vocabulary word best completes this sentence about "Remembrance"?
   The speaker in "Remembrance" decided not to mourn her dead beloved, because she still had to live her _____ life.

   A. languish
   B. rapturous
   C. gaunt
   D. terrestrial

_____ 13. Which vocabulary word best completes this sentence about "The Darkling Thrush?"
   The darkness and the trees _____ the speaker's view of the thrush.

   A. languished
   B. obscured
   C. prodded
   D. raptured

____ **14.** Which of the following sentences is correctly written in the active voice?
   A. The report will be written and edited tomorrow by me.
   B. The report will be written by me and edited by me tomorrow.
   C. I will write the report and it will be edited by me tomorrow.
   D. I will write and edit the report tomorrow.

Essay

15. Emily Brontë and Thomas Hardy use stanzas to present units of meaning, in the same way that paragraphs are used when writing prose. By linking the stanzas, they are able to develop the overall meaning of their poems. Both use the stanza structure to show irony. Choose one of the three poems, and write an essay in which you explain how the poet develops irony through the use of stanzas.

16. The three poems—"Remembrance," "The Darkling Thrush," and "Ah, Are You Digging on My Grave?"—present different attitudes toward life and death. With which poem do you most agree or disagree? In an essay, explain why you agree or disagree with the poem you chose. What ideas does it present that reflect your feelings or that you disagree with most strongly?

17. **Thinking About the Essential Question: Does a sense of place shape literature, or does literature shape a sense of place?** Select one of the three poems you have read in this grouping. Write an essay discussing the sense of place in the poem. How does the author create a sense of place for readers? What details does he use to contribute to the sense of place? Finally, what sense do you, as reader, get about the place that inspired the poem?

"Remembrance" by Emily Brontë
"The Darkling Thrush" and **"Ah, Are You Digging on My Grave?"** by Thomas Hardy
Selection Test B

Critical Reading *Identify the letter of the choice that best completes the statement or answers the question.*

____ 1. What does the speaker of "Remembrance" plan to do?
   A. build a monument to her love
   B. find a new love
   C. forget her love
   D. mourn her love until her own death

____ 2. What is the meaning of this stanza from "Remembrance"?
   Sweet Love of youth, forgive if I forget thee
   While the World's tide is bearing me along:
   Other desires and other hopes beset me,
   Hopes which obscure but cannot do thee wrong.
   A. The living must find a way to survive after a loss.
   B. After the death of a loved one, all hope is gone.
   C. We become disillusioned with age.
   D. Our hopes do injustice to the memory of the dead.

____ 3. What is ironic about the speaker's words by the end of "Remembrance"?
   A. The speaker feels joyful.
   B. The speaker has found a way to cherish life.
   C. The speaker is bitter and resentful.
   D. The speaker is also dead.

____ 4. Which words best describe the speaker of "Remembrance"?
   A. young and carefree
   B. angry and frightened
   C. resigned and reflective
   D. disillusioned and confused

____ 5. What is significant about the setting of "The Darkling Thrush"?
   A. It is the last night of the century.
   B. The speaker is lost.
   C. The speaker describes a bird sanctuary.
   D. It is almost dawn.

____ 6. What is the speaker's tone in these lines from "The Darkling Thrush"?
   . . . And every spirit upon earth / Seemed fervorless as I.
   A. resentful
   B. discouraged
   C. passionate
   D. skeptical

____ 7. "The Darkling Thrush" is ironic because
      A. the ending is humorous.
      B. the bird cannot be seen in the dark.
      C. the speaker feels hopeful.
      D. the mood changes unexpectedly.

____ 8. What is the central idea of "The Darkling Thrush"?
      A. the estrangement of humans from nature
      B. the mysterious renewal of nature
      C. human conflict with himself
      D. the inevitable defeat of hope

____ 9. What is the mood of the final lines of "The Darkling Thrush"?
      A. grateful celebration
      B. bitter pessimism
      C. cautious optimism
      D. curiosity

____ 10. In "Ah, Are You Digging on My Grave?" who is digging on the speaker's grave?
      A. her husband
      B. a relative
      C. an enemy
      D. her dog

____ 11. By connecting the main ideas in the stanzas of "Ah, Are You Digging on My Grave?" the reader
      A. discovers how the speaker died.
      B. realizes the poem's dark humor.
      C. discovers the poem's mood is sentimental.
      D. eliminates the poem's irony.

____ 12. "Ah, Are You Digging on My Grave?" is ironic because
      A. the reader expects someone to grieve.
      B. dogs are incapable of grief.
      C. the speaker is a dead person.
      D. the reader expects a surprise ending.

Vocabulary and Grammar

____ 13. Like the barren twigs, the darkling thrush is _____.
      A. languish
      B. rapturous
      C. gaunt
      D. terrestrial

____ 14. Rather than _____ for his deceased wife, the woman's husband soon remarries.
      A. languish
      B. rapturous
      C. gaunt
      D. terrestrial

____ 15. In a _____ voice, the young woman excitedly described her feelings for her love.
   A. languish
   B. rapturous
   C. gaunt
   D. terrestrial

____ 16. Which of the following sentences is written in the passive voice?
   A. Henry glared at Cecilia angrily and told her that he wanted his money.
   B. "I want my money," Henry said as he glared angrily at Cecilia.
   C. Henry was angered by when she refused to give him Cecilia his money
   D. Cecilia owed Henry money.

____ 17. Which of the following sentences is correctly written in the active voice?
   A. The report will be written and edited tomorrow by me.
   B. The report will be written by me and edited by me tomorrow.
   C. I will write the report and it will be edited by me tomorrow.
   D. I will write and edit the report tomorrow.

Essay

18. Although each stanza in a poem is a unit of meaning, the stanzas work together to convey the poem's overall idea. In an essay, explain how reading stanzas as units of meaning helps you arrive at a deeper meaning for the whole poem. Use examples from Brontë's and Hardy's poems to support your points.

19. Brontë has been classified as a Romantic and Hardy as a Naturalist. Romanticism celebrates nature's wildness, the human soul, and imagination, while Naturalism views individuals as governed by social and natural forces often beyond their control. In an essay, decide whether these poems represent the literary movements to which the poets are linked. Give evidence from the poems to support your opinion.

20. **Thinking About the Essential Question: Does a sense of place shape literature, or does literature shape a sense of place?** Select one of the three poems you have read in this grouping. Write an essay discussing how the author creates a sense of place in the poem and what you, as reader, picture as the original place that inspired the poem. How do you think the "literary" place and the "actual" place compare?

Vocabulary Warm-up Word Lists

Study these words from the above selections. Then, complete the activities.

Word List A

seared [SEERD] *v.* charred, scorched, or burned the surface
The chef <u>seared</u> the steak to seal in the juice.

flame [FLAYM] *v.* burn; ignite
The lighter fluid made it easy to <u>flame</u> the charcoal.

smudge [SMUHJ] *n.* a blotch or smear, often made by dirt
After eating the candy, the child had a <u>smudge</u> of chocolate on her chin.

fleet [FLEET] *adj.* swift; rapid or nimble
The <u>fleet</u> rabbit ran faster than the dog.

trod [TRAHD] *v.* walked on, over, or along; trampled
The hikers made a path when they <u>trod</u> through the meadow's tall grass.

smeared [SMEERD] *v.* spread or daubed on a surface, sometimes messily
The hunter <u>smeared</u> insect repellent on his face and arms.

shod [SHAHD] *v.* furnished with shoes
Horses have to be <u>shod</u> to protect their hooves.

toil [TOYL] *n* . exhausting labor or effort; hard work
The farm laborers were paid for their <u>toil</u> with cash and produce.

Word List B

grandeur [GRAN jer] *n.* quality or condition of being grand; magnificence
Mansions are built with large rooms to create a sense of <u>grandeur</u>.

renown [re NOWN] *n.* fame; the quality of being widely honored
The boxer's <u>renown</u> began when he won an Olympic gold medal.

rue [ROO] *n.* sorrow; regret
To their <u>rue</u>, the team had to forfeit the game when two players were hurt.

outran [owt RAN] *v.* ran faster than; exceeded
The third baseman <u>outran</u> the shortstop and caught the ball.

grieving [GREEV ing] *v.* expressing grief; mourning
The elderly man has been <u>grieving</u> since his wife died.

springs [SPRINGZ] *n.* sources, origins, or beginnings
His family and friends are the <u>springs</u> of his happiness.

flock [FLAHK] *v.* congregate or travel in a crowd
Crowds <u>flock</u> to the city parks for free outdoor concerts.

blight [BLYT] *n.* something that impairs growth or causes something to rot
Excessive rain caused a <u>blight</u> in the hay field.

Name _____ Date _____

Poetry of Gerard Manley Hopkins and A. E. Housman
Vocabulary Warm-up Exercises

Exercise A *Fill in the blanks using each word from Word List A only once.*

When a fire begins mysteriously, inspectors examine the site for

[1] _____ objects and clues that might show what made the building

[2] _____ . If arson is suspected, they will check out any

[3] _____ that could be a fingerprint or a footprint. Although not as reli-

able as fingerprints, patterns that reveal how a foot was [4] _____ can

sometimes lead police to a guilty party. An arsonist might not have worried about where

he or she [5] _____ , thinking any footprints would have burned away.

Inspectors will also test any flammable substance that seems to have been

[6] _____ on a surface. Hopefully, all this [7] _____ will

provide answers before a rainstorm arrives and, with one [8] _____ cloud-

burst, destroys needed evidence.

Exercise B *Rewrite each sentence so the underlined vocabulary word from Word List B is used in a logical way. Be sure to keep the vocabulary word in your revision.*

Example: When a king is crowned, no one expects <u>grandeur</u> at the ceremony.
   When a king is crowned, everyone expects <u>grandeur</u> at the ceremony.

1. The writer's <u>renown</u> was obvious since no one had ever heard of her.

   _____

2. "I shall feel <u>rue</u> that I ever met you," the lady said to the hero she loved.

   _____

3. She <u>outran</u> her teammates and came in last.

   _____

4. The <u>grieving</u> man was full of energy and laughter.

   _____

5. The <u>blight</u> on the roses made them look especially pretty.

   _____

6. Children <u>flock</u> happily to the dentist's office.

   _____

7. Books he never read were the filmmaker's <u>springs</u> of inspiration.

   _____

Name _____   Date _____

Read the following passage. Pay special attention to the underlined words. Then, read it again, and complete the activities. Use a separate sheet of paper for your written answers.

Before candles were invented, Egyptians used torches that were made of reeds <u>smeared</u> or thickly coated with melted tallow. When lit, the torches created a large flame that sometimes <u>seared</u> the hands of those who held them. Lighted pieces of reed and sparks also fell off the torches, burning the feet of those who weren't properly <u>shod</u>.

Candlewicks were developed by the Romans to make lighting safer. They put wicks in the rendered animal fat to create a means to slowly burn the suet. These first candles were used to light homes and places of worship. They also aided those who <u>trod</u> on foot at night.

Tallow was used in all candles until the Middle Ages when sweet-smelling beeswax was introduced. Beeswax candles did not produce dirty smoke that would cause a <u>smudge</u> on nearby walls or ceilings. Instead, when lighted, beeswax would <u>flame</u> pure and clean. However, these candles were expensive, and only the wealthy could afford them.

America's colonial women contributed to candle making when they discovered that boiling the grayish green berries of bayberry bushes produced a sweet-smelling wax that burned clean. However, extracting the wax from the bayberries was a tedious process that required a lot of <u>toil</u>. As a result, the bayberry candle quickly went out of fashion after a <u>fleet</u> period of popularity. It was quickly replaced in the late eighteenth century by the wax candle created from sperm whale oil. Harder than beeswax or tallow, this candle was in demand since it did not soften in the summer heat.

1. Circle the words that tell what <u>smeared</u> means. Name something that you might see being *smeared*.

2. Circle the words that tell what <u>seared</u> people's hands. Explain was *seared* means.

3. Circle the words that tell what happened when sparks fell on someone who wasn't properly <u>shod</u>. Then, tell what *shod* means.

4. Circle the words that tell how the people who used the candles <u>trod</u>. Then, tell where you might *trod*.

5. Circle the words that tell what produced the <u>smudge</u>. Tell where might you find a *smudge*.

6. Circle the words that tell when the beeswax would <u>flame</u> pure and clean. Then, describe something you've seen *flame*.

7. Circle the words that show that making bayberry candles required a lot of <u>toil</u>. Describe something you think requires a lot of *toil*.

8. Circle the words that tell that the bayberry candle had a <u>fleet</u> period of popularity. Then, tell what *fleet* means.

Poetry of Gerard Manley Hopkins and A. E. Housman
Reading Warm-up B

Read the following passage. Pay special attention to the underlined words. Then, read it again, and complete the activities. Use a separate sheet of paper for your written answers.

In a moment of <u>grandeur</u>, thinking it would be a magnificent gesture, a fan of Shakespeare named Eugene Scheifflin decided to import to North America, at his own expense, all the birds mentioned in Shakespeare's plays. He made the necessary arrangements, first collecting the birds in England. Then, he transported about 100 European starlings, the same number of sparrows, and about twenty other species by the dozens to Central Park in New York City.

Scheifflin thought this was a worthy tribute, an act of personal generosity that would bring him <u>renown</u>. It did bring him fame, but not in the way he expected. The birds arrived in 1890 before people understood what their impact would be. No one realized that introducing species that are not native to an area upsets the balance of nature. Many now have regrets and <u>rue</u> when they remember the day that Scheifflin made this sentimental gesture. Bird lovers began <u>grieving</u> soon after the starlings' habits became obvious, and native birds began dying off rapidly.

Starlings are stocky iridescent black birds with an aggressive nature. They are fierce competitors for nest cavities and frequently expel other bird species. As starlings became established across the continent, they would <u>flock</u> together by the hundreds or even thousands, filling trees and darkening the sky. Their ability to take over an area <u>outran</u> attempts to contain them.

The successful adaptation of starlings is believed to be responsible for a decline in native cavity-nesting bird populations. It is also considered a <u>blight</u> by some bird lovers who regard starlings as pests. The inspiration or <u>springs</u> of Scheifflin's idea may or may not have been self-serving, but the result wasn't the peaceful integration of species that he had intended.

1. Circle the words that help explain the meaning of <u>grandeur</u>. Then, describe a gesture that you think has *grandeur*.

2. Underline the nearby word that means the same as <u>renown</u>. Tell what might bring someone *renown*.

3. Circle the word in the sentence that is a synonym for <u>rue</u>. Rewrite the sentence using another word for *rue*.

4. Underline the phrase that gives the reason for the <u>grieving</u>. Describe a situation where you might find people *grieving*.

5. Circle the words that help explain the meaning of <u>flock</u>. Then, describe some creatures that might *flock* together.

6. Underline the word that gives a clue to the meaning of <u>outran</u>. Give an example of someone who *outran* something.

7. Circle the nearby word that means almost the same as <u>blight</u>. Tell why you think bird lovers considered starlings a *blight*.

8. Underline the word that means the same as <u>springs</u>. Then, rewrite the sentence using a synonym for *springs*.

"God's Grandeur" and **"Spring and Fall: To a Young Child"**
by Gerard Manley Hopkins
"To an Athlete Dying Young" and **"When I Was One-and-Twenty"**
by A. E. Housman

Literary Analysis: Rhythm and Meter

Rhythm is the alternation of strong and weak—or stressed and unstressed—syllables, which creates a flow or movement. **Meter** describes or "measures" rhythm when it follows a regular pattern. When poets or readers examine the meter of a poem, they "scan" the poem, marking stressed syllables with á mark and unstressed syllables with ˘ a mark.

The meter of a poem is measured in feet. A foot is a combination of two or more syllables, at least one of which is typically stressed. There are specific kinds of feet. Here are two examples.

Metrical Foot	Pattern of Syllables	Example
iamb	one unstressed, one stressed (˘´)	The time you won your town the race
trochee	one stressed, one unstressed (´˘)	It will come to such sights colder

Another way to measure and label meter is to count how many feet are in a line. In the iambic example in the chart, the line contains four iambic feet. Thus, the line is said to be in iambic *tetrameter*. The words *trimeter* and *pentameter* refer to lines of poetry with three feet and five feet, respectively.

Hopkins is known for experimenting with rhythm. He uses counterpoint rhythm, which consists of two opposing rhythms in one line of poetry. He also uses what he called "sprung rhythm," which he felt closely imitates the flow of natural speech. In sprung rhythm, each foot begins with a stressed syllable, which may then be followed by any number of unstressed syllables. Scanning a poem written in sprung rhythm reveals its lack of conventional meter.

DIRECTIONS: *Follow the instructions given to examine the meter of Hopkins's and Housman's poems. (Scansion is not an exact science, but you should be able to find general patterns.)*

1. Scan the second stanza of "To an Athlete Dying Young." Then, identify the meter of each line.

   Today, the road all runners come,
   Shoulder-high we bring you home,
   And set you at your threshold down,
   Townsman of a stiller town.

2. Scan these two lines from "God's Grandeur."

   And for all this, nature is never spent:
     There lives the dearest freshness deep down things; . . .

   What effect does the meter have on the meaning of these lines?

   _____

Name _____ Date _____

"God's Grandeur" and "Spring and Fall: To a Young Child"
by Gerard Manley Hopkins
"To an Athlete Dying Young" and **"When I Was One-and-Twenty"**
by A. E. Housman

Reading Strategy: Apply Biography

Knowing something about a poet can help readers understand that person's poetry more fully. Even simple details, such as knowing whether a poet is a man or a woman, can make a poem's meaning more clear. Whenever you read an author's **biography** in a textbook or anthology, be sure to apply what you learn to that person's writings.

Perhaps the most significant and startling fact about Gerard Manley Hopkins, for example, is that he was a Jesuit priest for all of his adult life. As you read his poems, look for signs of his religious beliefs. You may also see signs of the conflict he felt between his vocation and his other interests.

DIRECTIONS: *Use the charts on this page to record what you learn about each poet from the biographies on page 856. Then look for evidence of each man's character or personality in his poems. Quote lines or phrases from the poems that reveal the poets' backgrounds. An example entry has been provided.*

Characteristic of Hopkins	Where Characteristic Is Seen in Poems
strong religious beliefs	"The world is charged with the grandeur of God." ("God's Grandeur," line 1)

Characteristic of Housman	Where Characteristic Is Seen in Poems

Name _____ Date _____

"God's Grandeur" and "Spring and Fall: To a Young Child"
by Gerard Manley Hopkins
"To an Athlete Dying Young" and "When I Was One-and-Twenty"
by A. E. Housman
Vocabulary Builder

Using Coined Words

A. DIRECTIONS: *In "Spring and Fall," Hopkins uses* unleaving *to describe the falling of the leaves from the branches. This coined word concisely and descriptively expresses the poet's idea. For each of the following phrases, either coin a noun that names the idea or image in a descriptive way, or coin an adjective that would suit the subject.*

1. a puddle _____

2. the first leaf buds of spring _____

3. puppies _____

4. a playground full of children _____

Using the Word List

   blight   brink   grandeur   lintel   rue   smudge

B. DIRECTIONS: *Choose the letter of the word or phrase most nearly similar in meaning to each numbered word below. Write the letters on the lines provided.*

___ **1.** blight
    A. disease
    B. rotten
    C. dim
    D. understandable

___ **2.** grandeur
    A. more grand
    B. larger
    C. magnificence
    D. haughtiness

___ **3.** rue
    A. mourn
    B. rejoice
    C. blush
    D. regret

___ **4.** smudge
    A. thought
    B. wipe
    C. stain
    D. work of art

___ **5.** brink
    A. edge
    B. death
    C. sadness
    D. thought

___ **6.** lintel
    A. soup
    B. legume
    C. wooden frame
    D. bar above a door

"God's Grandeur" and "Spring and Fall: To a Young Child"
by Gerard Manley Hopkins
"To an Athlete Dying Young" and "When I Was One-and-Twenty"
by A. E. Housman

Integrated Language Skills: Support For Writing: Letter of Recommendation

You are Robert Bridges, and you are writing a letter to a British publishing company to recommend that it publish a book of Hopkins's poetry. Use the following chart to help you organize your thoughts on what is unique about Hopkins's poetry. Remember to describe these aspects of Hopkins's poetry in a positive way so that you will persuade the publisher to publish a book.

Hopkins's Innovative Style	What does it mean?	Examples from Hopkins's Poems	How will you describe it in your letter?
1. Sprung Rhythm			
2. Inscape			
3. Coined Words			

Name _____ Date _____

"God's Grandeur" and "Spring and Fall: To a Young Child"
by Gerard Manley Hopkins
"To an Athlete Dying Young" and "When I Was One-and-Twenty"
by A. E. Housman
Enrichment: Social Studies

Hopkins and Housman lived and worked in various cities in England, Wales, Scotland, and Ireland during their lifetimes. Modern-day readers often enjoy visiting the places where their favorite authors and poets lived and worked. This map identifies the locations of Hopkins's and Housman's activities.

DIRECTIONS: *Study the map. Then write general directions, using compass points, for modern-day visitors to travel from London to the specified points on the map.*

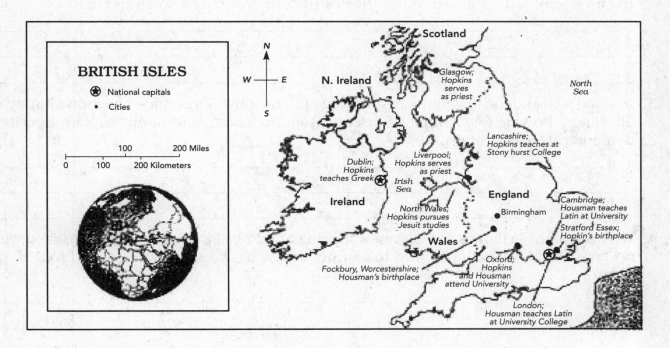

1. Send a traveler to tour places with which only A. E. Housman is connected. _____
_____

2. Send a traveler to learn more about Hopkins's work as a priest. _____
_____

3. Send another traveler to learn specifically about the childhoods of Hopkins and Housman.
_____

4. Where should a traveler go who wants to compare the college careers of the two poets? Give directions. _____
_____

5. Finally, send a traveler to learn about Hopkins's work in Ireland. _____
_____

Name _____ Date _____

Poems by Gerard Manley Hopkins and A. E. Housman
Open-Book Test

Short Answer *Write your responses to the questions in this section on the lines provided.*

1. How are Gerard Manley Hopkins's religious beliefs evident in the poem "God's Grandeur"?

   _____
   _____
   _____

2. Line 12 of "God's Grandeur" refers to the dawn of morning at sunrise. According to the poem, why does this instance of nature reflect the work of God?

   _____
   _____
   _____

3. In "God's Grandeur," Hopkins displays his philosophy of *inscape*—the individuality of all things. Provide an example of *inscape* from the poem, and briefly explain how it demonstrates this concept.

   _____
   _____
   _____

4. Why are some syllables in Hopkins's "Spring and Fall: To a Young Child" marked with accents? What is the term used to identify the type of metrical verse found in this poem?

   _____
   _____
   _____

5. How does the contrast of "spring and fall" in the title "Spring and Fall: To a Young Child" relate to the poem's meaning?

   _____
   _____
   _____

6. Use a single sentence to summarize A. E. Housman's poem "To an Athlete Dying Young" in your own words. Explain your answer, using examples from the poem.

   _____
   _____
   _____

7. Identify the term that indicates the number of feet per line in "To an Athlete Dying Young," and locate the lines in the poem that are trochaic.

   _____

   _____

   _____

8. Read line 12 of Housman's poem, "When I Was One-and-Twenty." What adjustment must the reader make to follow Housman's iambic trimeter and keep the rhythm of the meter?

   _____

   _____

   _____

9. Fill out the chart shown below to show the advice that the speaker receives in the first stanza of Housman's "When I Was One-and Twenty" and that he receives in the second stanza.

Advice in Stanza 1	Advice in Stanza 2

   How do you reconcile these two pieces of advice?

   _____

   _____

   _____

10. If a *blight* affected the crops, would the harvest be likely to be good? Explain why or why not.

   _____

   _____

   _____

Essay

Write an extended response to the question of your choice or to the question or questions your teacher assigns you.

11. Both Hopkins's "Spring and Fall: To a Young Child" and Housman's "To an Athlete Dying Young" are about human mortality. In an essay, compare and contrast how the two poets develop this theme. Which listeners are the speakers addressing? How are these listeners alike and different? Which speaker's sympathy is the most convincing? Use details from the poems to support your response.

12. In an essay, discuss the effect of the rhythms in Hopkins's poems "God's Grandeur" and "Spring and Fall: To a Young Child." Consider how the movement of the words affects the impact that the poems have on readers.

13. In an essay, discuss what you think A. E. Housman's purpose was for writing "To an Athlete Dying Young." Is it a tribute? Is it a simple statement? Is it a reflection of the poet's attitude toward life? Use examples from the poem to support your main points.

14. **Thinking About the Essential Question: Do writers gain more by accepting or by rejecting tradition?** In an essay, compare and contrast Gerald Manley Hopkins and A. E, Housman as traditional vs. innovative writers. What aspects of each poet's work are pioneering? What aspects might be described as traditional? Support your main ideas with specific references to the texts.

Oral Response

15. Go back to question 1, 3, 5, 6, 9, or the question your teacher assigns you. Take a few minutes to expand your answer and prepare an oral response. Find additional details in the selections that support your points. If necessary, make an outline to guide your oral response.

"God's Grandeur" and **"Spring and Fall: To a Young Child"** by Gerard Manley Hopkins
"To an Athlete Dying Young" and **"When I Was One-and-Twenty"** by A. E. Housman

Selection Test A

Critical Reading *Identify the letter of the choice that best answers the question.*

____ 1. Gerard Manley Hopkins was a Catholic priest. Which line from "God's Grandeur" most strongly suggests the depth of his faith?
A. "Generations have trod, have trod, have trod; / And all is seared with trade. . . ."
B. "Because the Holy Ghost over the bent / World broods with warm breast . . ."
C. "And for all this, nature is never spent; / There lives the dearest freshness . . ."
D. ". . . the soil / Is bare now, nor can foot feel, being shod."

____ 2. In "God's Grandeur," what does Hopkins mean when he refers to the "grandeur of God"?
A. people
B. education
C. poetry
D. nature

____ 3. What characteristic of counterpoint rhythm is illustrated in this line from "God's Grandeur"?
  And all is seared with trade; bleared, smeared with toil . . .
A. a regular pattern of stressed and unstressed syllables
B. a regular pattern of unstressed and stressed feet
C. Two opposing rhythms appear together.
D. All syllables are stressed.

____ 4. What is the child grieving over in "Spring and Fall: To a Young Child"?
A. becoming ill
B. the death of a friend
C. nature's changes
D. the death of parents

____ 5. What is the main idea of "Spring and Fall: To a Young Child"?
A. People are only young once.
B. All things die at some point.
C. Nature has cycles of birth and death.
D. Spring is a time of hope.

____ 6. What type of rhythm is used in this line from "To an Athlete Dying Young"?
  The time you won your town the race . . .
A. iambic
B. trochaic
C. anapestic
D. sprung

____ 7. What is the theme of "To an Athlete Dying Young"?
     A. the lasting peace of death
     B. the reasons for athletic competition
     C. the tragedy of an early death
     D. the glory of athletic achievement

____ 8. What advice is the speaker given in "When I Was One-and-Twenty"?
     A. Do not fall madly in love.
     B. Speak well of others.
     C. Do not tell people your true thoughts.
     D. Find someone to be your friend.

____ 9. Which line from "When I Was One-and-Twenty" includes a trochaic foot?
     A. "I heard a wise man say. . . ."
     B. "But keep your fancy free. . . ."
     C. "No use to talk to me."
     D. "'Tis paid with sighs a plenty. . . ."

Vocabulary and Grammar

____ 10. Which is the best *antonym* for *rue*, based on this line from "When I Was One-and-Twenty"?
     'Tis paid with sighs a plenty
     And sold for endless rue.

     A. sorrow
     B. reward
     C. joy
     D. regret

11. Which vocabulary word best completes the following sentence?
     There was a _____ on the ground where the man walked.
     A. brink
     B. grandeur
     C. lintel
     D. smudge

12. Which vocabulary word best completes the following sentence?
     I thought that I was on the _____ of disaster when I heard the thunder and saw the lightning.
     A. brink
     B. grandeur
     C. lintel
     D. smudge

13. Which of the following sentences uses a coined word?
     A. Bobby was struck speechless when he heard the news.
     B. Bobby was struck speechful when he heard the news.
     C. Bobby could not speak when he heard the news.
     D. Bobby could not stop speaking when he heard the news.

____ **14.** Which sentence contains an error in its capitalization of the compass point?

    A. After leaving Oxford, Houseman traveled southeast to London.

    B. Hopkins was born in Essex, a county to the east of London.

    C. Houseman grew up in Worcestershire, a region Northwest of London.

    D. Houseman wrote about the county of Shropshire in west central Britain.

Essay

15. Both "Spring and Fall: To a Young Child" and "To an Athlete Dying Young" are about human mortality. In an essay, compare how the poets develop this theme. Which listeners are the speakers addressing? How are these listeners alike and different? Which speaker's sympathy is the most convincing? Use details from the poems to support your response.

16. In an essay, explain Gerard Manley Hopkins's view of nature. What does he think should be people's relationship with nature? Give examples from Hopkins's poems to support your conclusions.

17. **Thinking About the Essential Question: Do writers gain more by accepting or rejecting tradition?** In an essay, compare and contrast the poems of Gerald Manley Hopkins and A. E. Houseman. First, identify the innovative poet and the traditional poet. Support your position by discussing what makes the poetry innovative or traditional. Then, discuss which style you enjoy more as a reader. Give reasons why one style appeals to you as opposed to the other.

"God's Grandeur" and **"Spring and Fall: To a Young Child"** by Gerard Manley Hopkins
"To an Athlete Dying Young" and **"When I Was One-and-Twenty"** by A. E. Housman
Selection Test B

Critical Reading *Identify the letter of the choice that best completes the statement or answers the question.*

_____ 1. Gerard Manley Hopkins's "God's Grandeur" contrasts
A. the flame of poetry with the oil of commerce.
B. the splendor of creation with the dullness of mankind.
C. western darkness with eastern light.
D. the sad wisdom of age with the fresh inexperience of youth.

_____ 2. What type of rhythm is used in this line from "Spring and Fall: To a Young Child"?
Áh! ás the heart grows older

A. trochaic rhythm
B. sprung rhythm
C. blank rhythm
D. iambic pentameter

_____ 3. What characteristic of counterpoint rhythm does this line from "God's Grandeur" illustrate?
World broods with warm breast and with ah! bright wings

A. a regular pattern of stressed syllables
B. the omission of prepositions as connectors
C. two opposing rhythms appearing together
D. the use of iambic tetrameter

_____ 4. Which of the lines from "God's Grandeur" is most indicative of Hopkins's religious faith?
A. "Because the Holy Ghost over the bent / World broods with warm breast and with ah! bright wings."
B. "Generations have trod, have trod, have trod; / And all is seared with trade . . ."
C. ". . . the soil / Is bare now, nor can foot feel, being shod."
D. "And for all this, nature is never spent; / There lives the dearest freshness deep down things;"

_____ 5. What event occasions Gerard Manley Hopkins's "Spring and Fall: To a Young Child"?
A. the destruction of a forest
B. the death of a child of a family friend
C. a child's sadness at fallen leaves
D. the death of a child's parents

_____ 6. In "Spring and Fall: To a Young Child," the image of "wanwood leafmeal" suggests the
A. bounty of harvest.
B. process of decay.
C. mystery of the forest.
D. innocence of childhood.

____ 7. Hopkins's profession as a priest may suggest an interpretation of "Spring and Fall: To a Young Child" that includes
  A. death as an inevitable, but not an evil, force.
  B. considering the child's feelings to be mistaken.
  C. the idea of "Fall" as original sin.
  D. regarding nature as a lesser power than God.

____ 8. "Spring and Fall: To a Young Child" is mostly about
  A. recognizing that all things die.
  B. the glory of divine grace.
  C. accepting a child's death.
  D. appreciating the four seasons.

____ 9. Which lines from "To an Athlete Dying Young" suggest that glory does not last?
  A. "The time you won your town the race / We chaired you through the market place;"
  B. "And early though the laurel grows / It withers quicker than the rose."
  C. "And silence sounds no worse than cheers / After earth has stopped the ears."
  D. "Eyes the shady night has shut / Cannot see the record cut."

____ 10. The tone of "When I Was One-and-Twenty" is _____.
  A. regretful.
  B. sarcastic.
  C. respectful.
  D. angry.

____ 11. In A. E. Housman's "When I Was One-and-Twenty," the line "I heard a wise man say" contains which kind of metrical foot?
  A. dactyl
  B. trochee
  C. iamb
  D. anapest

Vocabulary and Grammar

____ 12. The word *rue* means
  A. contempt.
  B. joy.
  C. shade.
  D. regret.

____ 13. In "To an Athlete Dying Young," Housman refers to "the rout / of lads that wore their honors out." A *rout* is
  A. a failed plan.
  B. a loud clamor.
  C. a traveled path.
  D. a disorderly mob.

_____ 14. A *blight* is a
  A. withering.
  B. fate.
  C. effort.
  D. radiance.

15. Identify the coined word(s) in the following excerpt from "Spring and Fall: To a Young Child."

    Though worlds of wanwood leafmeal lie

    And yet you will weep and know why.

  A. wanwood
  B. leafmeal
  C. wanwood and leafmeal
  D. though worlds

16. The word *smudge* means
  A. margin.
  B. lintel.
  C. smear.
  D. sorrow.

17. A *lintel* is a
  A. horizontal bar above a door.
  B. type of legume.
  C. kind of soup.
  D. vertical bar at the side of a door.

Essay

18. To make his point about early death, A. E. Housman might have chosen any young person as a symbol, before disappointment or corruption could mar life. Instead, he chose an athlete in "To an Athlete Dying Young." Why does an athlete emphasize Housman's theme especially well? Write an essay in which you explain what it is about an athlete that symbolizes Housman's points about time and life effectively. Use examples from the poem to illustrate your ideas.

19. The beauty of nature is keenly on Gerard Manley Hopkins's mind as he writes. In both "God's Grandeur" and "Spring and Fall: To a Young Child," scenes of natural beauty illustrate Hopkins's love of the world. Where, to Hopkins, do humans fit into the scene? Write an essay in which you discuss Hopkins's concept of humanity's relationship to nature, as revealed in the two poems of this section. Use examples from the poems to support your ideas.

20. **Thinking About the Essential Question: Do writers gain more by accepting or rejecting tradition?** In an essay, compare and contrast the poems of Gerald Manley Hopkins and A. E. Houseman by identifying which poet is more traditional and which is more innovative. Support your position with references to the poems. Then, discuss which style you enjoy more as a reader.

Writing Workshop—Unit 5
Integrating Grammar Skills

Revising Your Paragraphs

As you introduce blocks of information in your report, help the reader follow your train of thought from one paragraph to another. When you revise, **add transitions to improve the flow of ideas.** Transitional words and phrases show the relationships between ideas and clairfy the connections you want readers to make. The following chart shows common transitions used to show different kinds of relationships.

chronological order	first, next, recently, later, finally
comparison-and-contrast	both, like, unlike, however, on the other hand
cause-and-effect	as a result, therefore, because, thus
details that support a main idea	in addition, furthermore, for instance, for example, moreover

Adding Transitions

DIRECTIONS: *Copy the following paragraphs from a research report. Then revise the paragraphs by adding transitions where they are needed to show the relationships between ideas.*

Dickens in America

Charles Dickens made two trips to North America. In 1842, Dickens traveled with his wife to the United States and Canada. The journey was successful. Dickens created controversy by supporting the abolition of slavery. Dickens spent time in <u>New York City</u>. There he gave lectures and raised support for copyright laws. He recorded many of his impressions of America. He stayed there for one month. He met famous American authors such as <u>Washington Irving</u> and <u>William Cullen Bryant</u>.

Dickens made a trip to the United States in 1867. He spent most of this trip in New York. He gave 22 readings at <u>Steinway Hall</u> and four at <u>Plymouth Church of the Pilgrims</u>. He wrote about many significant changes he observed in the United States. His final appearance was at a banquet at <u>Delmonico</u>'s in 1868. There he promised to never criticize America again. Dickens boarded his ship to return to Britain on April 23, <u>1868</u>.

Writing Workshop—Unit 5
Reflective Essay: Revising Overall Structure

In an essay, to be sure to **maintain a balance between specific incidents or details and general ideas**. Specific events and details help set a scene or advance an idea. General ideas comment on or provide an interpretation of specific events. When you revise, add or eliminate details and general ideas as needed to maintain a balance.

Specific Incident: Every time I asked Al a question, he answered with another question.

General Idea: Gradually I understood that he was helping me reach my own conclusion.

A. DIRECTIONS: *Add three specific details to the following general idea.*

It is important to make a good first impression at a job interview.

_____

_____

_____

B. DIRECTIONS: *Add a general comment to sum up or interpret the details below.*

When rock climbing, think about the hazards. If you're a beginner, never go rock climbing without another person. Be sure to have the proper gear and beware of hypothermia.

_____

C. DIRECTIONS: *Read the following passage, noting the specific incidents and general ideas. Then, answer the questions.*

(1) For the first time, Cara felt that with her background in music production, she could contribute something of value to the band. (2) She was able to recommend a good studio and several excellent sound technicians. (3) She understood that her knowledge in this area served an important role (4) The way band members responded to her suggestions made her feel worthy.

1. Which sentence would you eliminate? _____

2. Why would you eliminate that sentence? _____

3. With what kind of sentence would you replace the eliminated sentence? _____

4. Suggest a sentence of your own that would serve the purpose. _____

Name _____ Date _____

Analyzing and Evaluating Entertainment Media

Choose an example of visual entertainment media—a movie, TV show, or Internet clip. Use this form to help you examine how the selection shapes content and viewer response.

Title (of movie, show, skit, etc.):
_____

Type of entertainment media:
_____

Summarize the story it tells:
_____
_____
_____

How does it appeal to cultural values?
_____
_____

Are there any stereotypes in this representation? Explain:
_____
_____

Explain how any *two* of the following techniques are used to tell the story and shape response: *special effects, editing, camera angles, reaction shots, sequencing,* or *music.*

Technique 1:
_____
_____
_____

Technique 2:
_____
_____
_____
_____

Unit 5 Vocabulary Workshop
Idioms

Idioms—expressions that are not taken literally—can add vividness, convey character, and set a mood in speaking and writing. English is full of unique and lively idioms. Good writers, however, avoid those idioms that have become overused and trite.

A. DIRECTIONS: *Identify the overused idiom in each sentence. Then rewrite the sentence with original words and phrases.*

  Example: In his speech, the senator hit the nail right on the head.

  Rewrite: In his speech, the senator's analysis of the situation was absolutely
      accurate.

1. This movie is as dull as dishwater.

  _____

2. Bring up that topic again and you will be beating a dead horse.

  _____

3. If he loses his job, he will really be up the creek.

  _____

4. They remained together through thick and thin.

  _____

5. Who wears the pants in that family?

  _____

B. DIRECTIONS: *Rewrite the following paragraph, replacing the overused idioms with original words and phrases.*

Everyone thought he was a long shot to win the election. Most of the political insiders would not touch him with a ten-foot pole. However, he came out of the financial scandal smelling like a rose. They had assumed he was at the end of his rope, but they just were not able to see the forest for the trees.

_____

_____

_____

_____

_____

_____

_____

_____

_____

Essential Questions Workshop—Unit 5

In their poems, fiction, and nonfiction works, the writers in Unit Five express ideas that relate to the three Essential Questions framing this book. Review the literature in the unit. Then, for each Essential Question, choose an author and at least one passage from the author's writing that expresses an idea related to the question. Use this chart to complete your work.

Essential Question	Author/Selection	Literary Passage
What is the relationship between place and literature?		
How does literature shape or reflect society?		
What is the relationship of the writer to tradition?		

Unit 5: Progress and Decline
Benchmark Test 9

MULTIPLE CHOICE

Literary Analysis and Reading Skills *Answer the following questions.*

1. Which of the following elements is an aspect of many nineteenth-century novels?
   A. a simple plot
   B. social criticism
   C. the absence of minor characters
   D. dramatic irony

2. In comparing and contrasting the speakers of Victorian poems, which statement is most accurate?
   A. Most of the speakers have lost faith in love.
   B. The speakers are invariably optimistic and patriotic.
   C. Some speakers are hopeful, whereas others tend to be pessimistic.
   D. Unlike the speakers of lyric poems, the speakers of dramatic monologues are hesitant.

3. Which of these statements is true about a poem that uses sprung rhythm?
   A. It uses iambic pentameter.
   B. All feet begin with a stressed syllable.
   C. Two opposing rhythms appear together in the same line.
   D. Lines of trochaic trimeter alternate with lines of trochaic tetrameter.

4. Which of these statements use emotive language as a mode of persuasion?
   A. Seen from space, the earth looks like a blue ball.
   B. Our planet is mostly water but contains masses of land.
   C. Scientists study species to determine which have become extinct.
   D. Pollution is a cruel example of what humankind has done to mother earth.

5. Which of these details about a Web site can best help you predict the credibility of its contents?
   A. the sponsor of the site
   B. the number of visitors to the site
   C. the date on which the site was last updated
   D. the number of headings and graphics used by the site

Read this poem. Then, answer the questions that follow.

> Oh, to be in England
> Now that April's there,
> And whoever wakes in England
> Sees, some morning, unaware,

5   That the lowest boughs and the brushwood sheaf
        Round the elm-tree bole are in tiny leaf,
        While the chaffinch sings on the orchard bough
        In England—now!

        "Home-Thoughts, from Abroad" by Robert Browning

6. Which word best describes the mood of the poem?
   A. joyous
   B. longing
   C. bitter
   D. sad

7. What inference can you make about the speaker based on the details of the poem?
   A. The speaker is a naturalist.
   B. The speaker is not Robert Browning.
   C. The speaker wishes he were English.
   D. The speaker misses England.

8. Judging from the details and mood of the poem, choose the statement that best expresses its theme.
   A. Unlike animals, human beings can appreciate the natural wonders all around them.
   B. Missing a beautiful time in one's native land can make a person homesick.
   C. Spring is the season of renewal, when human beings are most hopeful.
   D. England is a unique country, unlike any other in the world.

9. How many end-stopped lines does the poem contain?
   A. three
   B. four
   C. five
   D. eight

Read this poem. Then, answer five questions that follow.

        Oh, when I was in love with you,
          Then I was clean and brave,
        And miles around the wonder grew
          How well did I behave.
5   And now the fancy passes by,
          And nothing will remain,
        And miles around they'll say that I
          Am quite myself again.

        "On, When I Was in Love with You" by A. E. Housman

10. What makes the ending of the poem ironic?
    A. It has a speaker
    B. It has a silent listener.
    C. The speaker and the poet are the same.
    D. The speaker draws a dramatic conclusion.

11. What makes the ending of the poem ironic?
    A. It is at variance with readers' expectations.
    B. It suggests that love is just a whim.
    C. It uses a figure of speech.
    D. It uses humor.

12. How does the stanza structure clarify the central meaning of the poem?
    A. The first stanza is hopeful, and the second is wistful.
    B. The first stanza describes the past, and the second describes the present.
    C. The first stanza describes the present, and the second describes the future.
    D. The first stanza expresses romantic hopes, and the second reveals everyday reality.

13. From the details, what inference can you make about the speaker of the poem?
    A. The speaker falls in love frequently.
    B. The speaker is able to poke fun at himself.
    C. The speaker is an unpleasant, bitter person.
    D. The speaker expects the listener to take him back.

14. Which choice best describes the poem's meter?
    A. Lines of iambic pentameter alternate with lines of iambic tetrameter.
    B. Lines of iambic tetrameter alternate with lines of iambic trimeter.
    C. Lines of trochaic tetrameter alternate with lines of trochaic trimeter.
    D. Lines of trochaic tetrameter alternate with lines of iambic tetrameter.

In this passage from a novel by Charles Dickens, the main character has recently been placed in a workhouse for the poor. Read the passage. Then, answer the questions that follow.

Poor Oliver! He little thought, as he lay sleeping in happy unconsciousness of all around him, that the board had that very day arrived at a decision which would exercise the most material influence over all his future fortunes. But they had. And this was it:

The members of this board were very sage, deep, philosophical men; and when they came to turn their attention to the workhouse, they found out at once, what ordinary folks would never have discovered—the poor people like it! . . . "Oho!" said the board, looking very knowing; "we are the fellows to set this to rights; we'll stop it all, in no time." So, they established the rule, that all poor people should have the alternative (for they would compel nobody, not they) of being starved by a gradual process in the house, or by a quick one out of it. With this view, they contracted with the waterworks to lay on an unlimited supply of water; and with a corn factory to supply periodically small quantities of oatmeal; and issued three meals of thin gruel a day, with an onion twice a week, and half a roll on Sundays.

Oliver Twist by Charles Dickens

Name _____ Date _____

15. What social issue from the novel's historical period does this passage examine?
    A. an insufficient diet
    B. a widespread water shortage
    C. the adoption of laws governing orphans
    D. the practice of housing the poor in workhouses

16. What example of irony does the passage contain?
    A. Although new to the workhouse, Oliver plays a central role in events that unfold there.
    B. Board members are expected to care about the poor but instead treat them harshly.
    C. The poor are expected to hate living in the workhouse, but they like living there.
    D. The waterworks supplies unlimited water, but the board limits the portions of gruel.

17. What seems to be the writer's chief purpose in this passage?
    A. to entertain readers with amusing ironies concerning workhouse life
    B. to recount entertaining events in the life of the main character, Oliver Twist
    C. to inform readers of the ingredients of gruel and its role in the British diet
    D. to expose a social problem and persuade readers to help correct it

18. What belief seems to govern the political or philosophical assumptions underlying this passage?
    A. In a competitive society, only the fittest survive.
    B. Society has a moral obligation to help the needy.
    C. All people are equal under the laws of society.
    D. The British Empire is marked by its superiority.

19. Information about which aspect of the author's life can best help a reader understand and analyze the beliefs reflected in this passage?
    A. the hardships he experienced as a child
    B. his early career as a newspaper journalist
    C. his unprecedented success as a novelist
    D. the difficulties he experienced in his marriage

Vocabulary

20. Which sentence uses the italicized word figuratively?
    A. I like to *dance* the tango.
    B. The lord and lady attended a *dance*.
    C. Poets *dine* on love.
    D. We *dine* at twelve o'clock.

21. Based on your knowledge of the Latin suffix -ence, what kind of person would you say displays *beneficence*?
    A. someone who gives to charity
    B. someone who speaks clearly
    C. someone who harms others
    D. someone who changes his or her mind

22. Based on your knowledge of the Greek prefix *mono-*, choose the best definition of *monotone*.
    A. an ugly sound
    B. a duet
    C. an unchanging tone of voice
    D. a tuning chord

23. Which choice provides an accurate meaning and origin of the word *macadam*?
    A. a type of pavement, named for the person who invented it
    B. a type of apple, named for the botanist who first bred it
    C. a type of plaid, named for the clan whose members first wore it
    D. a type of lined paper, named for the teacher who popularized it

24. Which choice best describes someone who has *dominion* over others?
    A. a benevolent queen
    B. a harsh tyrant
    C. a court jester
    D. a clever actor

25. Which of the following best defines a coined word?
    A. a word meaning "money"
    B. a word that has been made up
    C. a word that is poetic
    D. a word that has been defined

Grammar

26. In which sentence are the verb tenses used correctly?
    A. When it snowed, the electricity goes out.
    B. When it has snowed, the electricity will go out.
    C. When it snowed, the electricity went out.
    D. When it snows, the electricity has gone out.

27. Which choice accurately expresses this sentence in the active voice?

    We were beaten by the Raiders in the last inning.

    A. Our team was beaten by the Raiders in the last inning.
    B. We were demolished by the Raiders in the last inning.
    C. In the last inning, we were beaten by the Raiders.
    D. The Raiders beat us in the last inning.

ESSAY

28. Write a biographical essay about a Victorian poet or novelist. Stress the relationship between the writer's life and the works he or she produced.

29. What poet would you recommend to a poet's hall of fame? Write a recommendation of a poet whose work and life you admire. Base your choice on both the writer's poetry and his or contribution to society, citing examples to support your choice.

30. Write an essay about the effect of fiction on society. Focusing on the past, cite examples of the way in which particular social issues have been portrayed in fiction. Then, discuss whether or not fiction had a role in changing society's views and practices regarding those issues.

Diagnostic Tests and Vocabulary in Context
Use and Interpretation

The Diagnostic Tests and Vocabulary in Context were developed to assist teachers in making the most appropriate assignment of *Prentice Hall Literature* program selections to students. The purpose of these assessments is to indicate the degree of difficulty that students are likely to have in reading/comprehending the selections presented in the *following* unit of instruction. Tests are provided at six separate times in each in each grade level—a *Diagnostic Test* (to be used prior to beginning the year's instruction) and a *Vocabulary in Context*, the final segment of the Benchmark Test appearing at the end of each of the first five units of instruction. Note that the tests are intended for use not as summative assessments for the prior unit, but as guidance for assigning literature selections in the upcoming unit of instruction.

The structure of all Diagnostic Tests and Vocabulary in Context in this series is the same. All test items are four-option, multiple-choice items. The format is established to assess a student's ability to construct sufficient meaning from the context sentence to choose the only provided word that fits both the semantics (meaning) and syntax (structure) of the context sentence. All words in the context sentences are chosen to be "below-level" words that students reading at this grade level should know. All answer choices fit *either* the meaning or structure of the context sentence, but only the correct choice fits *both* semantics and syntax. All answer choices—both correct answers and incorrect options—are key words chosen from specifically taught words that will occur in the subsequent unit of program instruction. This careful restriction of the assessed words permits a sound diagnosis of students' current reading achievement and prediction of the most appropriate level of readings to assign in the upcoming unit of instruction.

The assessment of vocabulary in context skill has consistently been shown in reading research studies to correlate very highly with "reading comprehension." This is not surprising as the format essentially assesses comprehension, albeit in sentence-length "chunks." Decades of research demonstrate that vocabulary assessment provides a strong, reliable prediction of comprehension achievement—the purpose of these tests. Further, because this format demands very little testing time, these diagnoses can be made efficiently, permitting teachers to move forward with critical instructional tasks rather than devoting excessive time to assessment.

It is important to stress that while the Diagnostic and Vocabulary in Context were carefully developed and will yield sound assignment decisions, they were designed to *reinforce*, not supplant, teacher judgment as to the most appropriate instructional placement for individual students. Teacher judgment should always prevail in making placement—or indeed other important instructional—decisions concerning students.

Diagnostic Tests and Vocabulary in Context
Branching Suggestions

These tests are designed to provide maximum flexibility for teachers. Your *Unit Resources* books contain the 40-question **Diagnostic Test** and 20-question **Vocabulary in Context** tests. At *PHLitOnline,* you can access the Diagnostic Test and complete 40-question Vocabulary in Context tests. Procedures for administering the tests are described below. Choose the procedure based on the time you wish to devote to the activity and your comfort with the assignment decisions relative to the individual students. Remember that your judgment of a student's reading level should always take precedence over the results of a single written test.

Feel free to use different procedures at different times of the year. For example, for early units, you may wish to be more confident in the assignments you make—thus, using the "two-stage" process below. Later, you may choose the quicker diagnosis, confirming the results with your observations of the students' performance built up throughout the year.

The **Diagnostic Test** is composed of a single 40-item assessment. Based on the results of this assessment, make the following assignment of students to the reading selections in Unit 1:

Diagnostic Test Score	Selection to Use
If the student's score is 0–25	more accessible
If the student's score is 26–40	more challenging

Outlined below are the three basic options for administering **Vocabulary in Context** and basing selection assignments on the results of these assessments.

1. For a one-stage, quicker diagnosis using the *20-item* test in the *Unit Resources:*

Vocabulary in Context Test Score	Selection to Use
If the student's score is 0–13	more accessible
If the student's score is 14–20	more challenging

2. If you wish to confirm your assignment decisions with a *two-stage* diagnosis:

Stage 1: Administer the 20-item test in the *Unit Resources*	
Vocabulary in Context Test Score	Selection to Use
If the student's score is 0–9	more accessible
If the student's score is 10–15	(Go to Stage 2.)
If the student's score is 16–20	more challenging

Stage 2: Administer items 21–40 from *PHLitOnline*	
Vocabulary in Context Test Score	Selection to Use
If the student's score is 0–12	more accessible
If the student's score is 13–20	more challenging

3. If you base your assignment decisions on the full 40-item **Vocabulary in Context** from *PHLitOnline:*

Vocabulary in Context Test Score	Selection to Use
If the student's score is 0–25	more accessible
If the student's score is 26–40	more challenging

Grade 12—Benchmark Test 9
Interpretation Guide

Skill Objective	Old Test Item Number	New Test Item Number	Reading Kit
Literary Analysis			
Speaker of Poem	2, 6, 13		pp. 204, 205
Meter, Free-Verse, and Blank Verse	3, 14		pp. 130, 131
Mood as a Key to Theme	6, 8		pp. 134, 135
The Novel and Social Criticism	1, 15, 16		pp. 138, 139
Dramatic Monologue	2, 10		pp. 58, 59
Poetic Structure: Theme and Irony	11, 12		pp. 156, 157
End-stopped Lines	8		pp. 70, 71
Reading Skill			
Predict Content, Purpose, and Organization	5		pp. 166, 167
Analyze Author's Philosophical Assumptions and Beliefs	17, 19		pp. 6, 7
Compare and Contrast Elements	2		pp. 38, 39
Historical Context	15		pp. 98, 99
Recognizing the Writer's Purpose	16		pp. 238, 239
Distinguishing Emotive and Informative Language	4		pp. 48, 49
Analyze Patterns of Organization	12		pp. 10, 11
Vocabulary			
Words with Literal and Figurative Meanings	20		pp. 302, 303
Latin Suffixes: -ence	21		pp. 290, 291
Greek Prefixes: mono-	22		pp. 256, 257
Etymology: macadam	23		pp. 250, 251
Word Phrase relationships	24		pp. 304, 305
Coined Words	25		pp. 248, 249
Grammar			
Avoiding shifts in verb tense	26		pp. 316, 317
Active and Passive Voice	27		pp. 308, 309
Writing			
Written Recommendation	28		n/a
Research Plan	29		n/a
Biographical Essay	30		pp. 346, 347

ANSWERS

Unit 5 Introduction

Names and Terms to Know, p. 5

A. 1. D; 2. G; 3. A; 4. I; 5. C; 6. B; 7. E; 8. J; 9. F; 10. H

B. Sample Answers

1. The Second Reform Bill of 1867 gave the vote to nearly one million new voters, mostly urban workingmen.

2. During the Victorian Age, Britain acquired Hong Kong, took direct control of India, and expanded its influence in Africa, gaining control of the Suez Canal and colonizing Kenya, Uganda, Nigeria, and Rhodesia.

3. Realist writers of the age included Charles Dickens, Anthony Trollope, Samuel Butler, George Meredith, and William Makepeace Thackeray.

4. The Pre-Raphaelite Brotherhood, founded by painter and poet Dante Gabriel Rossetti, rejected conventional art and sought a greater purity or "truth to nature." The group turned to medieval painters as models—artists who predated the great Italian master, Raphael.

Focus Questions, p. 6

Sample Answers

1. Britain ranked at the top of manufacturing nations worldwide. The ready availability of a large variety of low-cost goods encouraged the development of the working class and of a modern middle class.

2. Colonists could provide the mother country with raw materials and new markets. Britons feared that if they failed to seize a territory it would be colonized by one of their European rivals. Finally, the British felt that their brand of Western civilization was superior to the indigenous cultures of the areas they colonized.

3. Novels appealed to the middle class because this class contained many avid readers who were eager to read stories that reflected the major social issues of the day. Magazines played an important role in the publication of novels, since many novels appeared in serialized form in periodicals.

from In Memoriam, A.H.H., "The Lady of Shalott," "Ulysses," and "Tears, Idle Tears"
by Alfred, Lord Tennyson

Vocabulary Warm-up Exercises, p. 8

A. 1. wanes
2. idle
3. smite
4. feigned
5. vexed
6. wrought
7. discerning
8. remote

B. Sample Answers

1. Flowers prosper if you keep them watered and fertilized. The Andersons enjoy a prosperous lifestyle.

2. Jerry wants to put a casement in the wall facing the fountain. Meredith opened the casement and breathed in the fresh salt air.

3. The child's countenance revealed that she was happy to see her cousin. Your countenance would be improved with a smile.

4. Dan is on the verge of buying a new computer. Wanda planted daffodils on the verge of the garden.

5. Exercise prudence before swimming in a swift river. The prudent thing to do is to wait until the dress goes on sale.

6. Jeff gave Doris a yearning look. Maria yearns for the good old days.

7. The losing team decided to yield without finishing the game. Hazel was determined not to yield to the temptation of eating a piece of the chocolate cake before dinner.

Reading Warm-up A, p. 9

Sample Answers

1. faraway; The campsite is in a remote area of the forest.
2. (hard blow); *Smite* means "to strike or hit very hard."
3. doing nothing but resting; *busy*
4. (annoyed); I was vexed when my friend Susan kept pestering me to lend her my new necklace.
5. (pretended); Sam feigned interest in Beth's dog because he wanted to get to know her.
6. growing weaker; *strengthens*
7. (beautifully fashioned); A finely wrought item I own is an antique violin that was given to me by my Aunt Jane.
8. recognized what was happening; A piece of art that a discerning person might enjoy is a hand-blown glass vase.

Reading Warm-up B, p. 10

Sample Answers

1. thrive; If you want a garden to prosper, you have to water and weed it.
2. (predicted); The heavy gray clouds made it easy to forecast rain.
3. (window); *Casement* means "window that opens like a door."
4. (longing); *hoping*
5. good judgment; I try to exercise prudence by saving up for something rather than borrowing the money to buy it.
6. (looking up at her); A person who has just received some very happy news would have a countenance with a big smile on it.
7. the temptation to see Guinevere; *Yield* means "to give in to."

8. about to say goodbye; Perry was on the verge of telling Carol's secret.

Literary Analysis: The Speaker in Poetry, p. 11

Sample Answers

1. Ulysses reveals his impatience with the domestic duties of kingship and his need for action in order to stay "honed like a sword's cutting edge."

2. Ulysses's affectionate, confident tone is intended to inspire confidence and good feelings both in his son and among his subjects. Words like *well-loved, discerning,* and *fulfill* have connotations that can help create a positive atmosphere for transfer of power.

3. Ulysses speaks to his loyal followers, reminding them of the good and bad times they have shared on their adventures. Calling them "my mariners," he appeals strongly to their feelings of loyalty and to their spirits rather than to their physical natures. This is wise on Ulysses's part because his followers are old men now and have naturally declined in physical prowess.

4. Ulysses here speaks both to himself and to his mariners, offering them a chance to regain the difficult but satisfying life of forward motion and excitement they once knew. Having convinced them of the futility of remaining on the island, he holds out the appealing image of the "newer world" and the environment of the "sounding furrows" in which the men could once more take a vital, active role.

Reading Strategy: Analyze Author's Assumptions and Beliefs, p. 12

Sample Answers

1. Speaker is amazed that after the grief of losing a friend, there is a bright side; a benefit/Human beings grow and learn from their experiences.

2. Speaker is longing for days gone by./In longing for the past, we are grieving, just as we do when someone dies.

3. The speaker wants to travel again./Every experience changes us and helps us grow.

Vocabulary Builder, p. 13

A. 1. clasp / grip / join together with
   2. dance / to move feet and body rhythmically to music / grapple with

B. 1. C; 2. B; 3. D; 4. A; 5. B; 6. D; 7. B.

Enrichment: Culture, p. 15

Sample Answers

1. A classically educated person would share a detailed knowledge of literature, history, and religion with writers and thinkers from various times, and would also have a strong grasp of grammar.

2. The obvious advantages of a modern curriculum include highly specialized knowledge, a broader range of study, technical capability, and preparation for a career in a field of choice.

3. Some schools offer classical languages, and an emphasis on foreign language and literary studies is a remnant of classical education, as is the idea of a rounded, balanced body of knowledge that everyone should possess.

4. Classical studies offer a fundamental knowledge of the history of western civilization. The basic underpinnings of language, law, political science, and society owe their beginnings to classical knowledge.

Poetry of Alfred, Lord Tennyson

Open-Book Test, p. 16

Short Answer

1. "Far off thou art, but ever nigh:/I have thee still, and I rejoice." These lines tell us that the poet has decided his friend is still with him, even though the friend has died, and this conclusion makes the poet rejoice. Students may choose other lines and support their positions.
   Difficulty: *Average*   **Objective:** *Interpretation*

2. The poet suggests that great love can bring grief, but grief is worth the risk when the love is strong. Students' evaluations of this belief will vary. Be sure that students rely on a clear understanding of the poet's beliefs, as well as on specific experiences and observations from their own life.
   Difficulty: *Average*   **Objective:** *Reading*

3. Love lasts even after death.
   Difficulty: *Easy*   **Objective:** *Interpretation*

4. "Who is this? And what is here?" (line 163). The people at Camelot say this line. It places the reader in the crowd at Camelot, bringing him or her closer to the action.
   Difficulty: *Challenging*   **Objective:** *Literary Analysis*

5. The speaker believes that knights are loyal and true, which is the traditional view.
   Difficulty: *Average*   **Objective:** *Literary Analysis*

6. Tennyson tries to convey the belief that society tends to isolate artists.
   Difficulty: *Easy*   **Objective:** *Reading*

7. The poet portrays the happiness and freshness of young love and then contrasts these qualities with the nostalgia for days that are no more. Tennyson's language evokes longings for the past. Students' evaluations will vary. Be sure that students rely on a clear understanding of the poet's message and that they support their evaluations.
   Difficulty: *Average*   **Objective:** *Interpretation*

8. The speaker of the poem is Ulysses himself. The use of the pronoun "I" indicates a first-person point of view, and references to travel, the sea, roaming, and battling at Troy allude to Homer's *Odyssey*. Ulysses' conflict is that he has grown old, but he longs for the challenge of his adventures.
   Difficulty: *Easy*   **Objective:** *Literary Analysis*

9. He feels that his life has been based on the adventures that he has had and that these adventures have become part of who he is. Without adventuring further, the opportunities of the world are fading as he ages.

   Difficulty: *Average*   **Objective:** *Interpretation*

10. It is decreasing, because *waning* means "growing smaller."

    Difficulty: *Average*   **Objective:** *Vocabulary*

Essay

11. Students may choose "Ulysses" because they prefer the message of living life to the fullest to the idea of sitting still and gathering rust as though life becomes useless after a certain age. Other students may select the message conveyed in *In Memoriam, A. H. H.* because of all it says about friendship and how friendship can survive even death.

    Difficulty: *Easy*   **Objective:** *Essay*

12. The Lady floats away in a boat during a storm and freezes to death. Students should cite details from Part IV of the poem that indicate the Lady's fate.

    Difficulty: *Average*   **Objective:** *Essay*

13. Students will probably note the sadness and nostalgia associated with death, dying, and growing old that is present in all the poems. They should cite appropriate examples and use personal experience and coherent reasons and examples to evaluate Tennyson's ideas.

    Difficulty: *Challenging*   **Objective:** *Essay*

14. Students' responses will vary. Some students will see Tennyson's generally elegiac tone as typical of Victorian society and values; other students will cast the poet as more of an innovator, given his wide-ranging stylistic effects and choice of subjects. Evaluate students' essays on clarity, coherence, and specific support from the texts.

    Difficulty: *Average*   **Objective:** *Essay*

Oral Response

15. Oral responses should be clear, well organized, and well supported by appropriate details from the selections.

    Difficulty: *Average*   **Objective:** *Oral Interpretation*

Selection Test A, p. 19

Critical Reading

1. **ANS:** C	**DIF:** Easy	**OBJ:** Interpretation
2. **ANS:** D	**DIF:** Easy	**OBJ:** Interpretation
3. **ANS:** B	**DIF:** Easy	**OBJ:** Literary Analysis
4. **ANS:** A	**DIF:** Easy	**OBJ:** Comprehension
5. **ANS:** D	**DIF:** Easy	**OBJ:** Comprehension
6. **ANS:** A	**DIF:** Easy	**OBJ:** Reading Strategy
7. **ANS:** A	**DIF:** Easy	**OBJ:** Interpretation
8. **ANS:** C	**DIF:** Easy	**OBJ:** Interpretation

9. **ANS:** B	**DIF:** Easy	**OBJ:** Literary Analysis
10. **ANS:** C	**DIF:** Easy	**OBJ:** Comprehension

Vocabulary and Grammar

11. **ANS:** D	**DIF:** Easy	**OBJ:** Vocabulary
12. **ANS:** C	**DIF:** Easy	**OBJ:** Vocabulary
13. **ANS:** D	**DIF:** Easy	**OBJ:** Grammar

Essay

14. Students may choose "Ulysses" because they prefer the belief that life should be lived to the fullest to the idea of sitting still and gathering rust as though life becomes useless after a certain age. Others may think the belief conveyed in *In Memoriam* has lasting significance because of all it says about friendship and how it survives even death.

    Difficulty: *Easy*

    Objective: *Reading Strategy*

15. Students may or may not agree that "The Lady of Shalott" is about the life of an artist. Those who agree will point out that the Lady of Shalott is a weaver, a kind of artist, who looks at life through a mirror and tries to capture what she sees in her weaving. Her isolation and her fate when she tries to give up her isolated life and live in the real world might symbolize the fate of artists who try to live in the world as ordinary people.

    Difficulty: *Easy*

    Objective: *Essay*

16. Student answers will vary. Some students will see Tennyson as a conservative because of his tone and typical Victorian values. Others will argue that his choice of subjects and his style make him innovative. Answers should be well supported.

    Difficulty: *Average*

    Objective: *Essay*

Selection Test B, p. 22

Critical Reading

1. **ANS:** A	**DIF:** Easy	**OBJ:** Comprehension
2. **ANS:** B	**DIF:** Average	**OBJ:** Reading Strategy
3. **ANS:** D	**DIF:** Easy	**OBJ:** Literary Analysis
4. **ANS:** C	**DIF:** Easy	**OBJ:** Interpretation
5. **ANS:** A	**DIF:** Average	**OBJ:** Interpretation
6. **ANS:** C	**DIF:** Average	**OBJ:** Literary Analysis
7. **ANS:** B	**DIF:** Average	**OBJ:** Comprehension
8. **ANS:** B	**DIF:** Average	**OBJ:** Reading Strategy
9. **ANS:** D	**DIF:** Average	**OBJ:** Interpretation
10. **ANS:** A	**DIF:** Challenging	**OBJ:** Reading Strategy

11. ANS: C	DIF: Average	OBJ: Comprehension
12. ANS: D	DIF: Challenging	OBJ: Literary Analysis
13. ANS: A	DIF: Challenging	OBJ: Interpretation

Vocabulary and Grammar

14. ANS: D	DIF: Average	OBJ: Grammar
15. ANS: B	DIF: Easy	OBJ: Grammar
16. ANS: C	DIF: Easy	OBJ: Vocabulary
17. ANS: B	DIF: Average	OBJ: Vocabulary

Essay

18. Students should note that the type of heroism proposed by Tennyson is a heroism of effort rather than of accomplishment. Tennyson's Ulysses is no longer beautiful, young, strong, or hopeful. He has accomplished what one can accomplish and lists the accomplishments, including pride in his son. His heroism lies in making attempts, not what he is attempting, and to that end he will "sail beyond the sunset . . . until I die."

Difficulty: *Average*
Objective: *Essay*

19. Students should note that these four sections of the poem represent a progression from total grief to a kind of faith. Sections 1 and 7 illustrate the bleak impact of loss. Section 7 illustrates pain itself, as the speaker stands grieving in front of the house of his lost friend in the rain after a sleepless night. By Section 82, the speaker accepts death as an "Eternal process moving on." He indicates a surviving faith by describing A.H.H. as a "ruined chrysalis." A chrysalis is ruined by an emerging butterfly; therefore, death leads to a more beautiful form of life. In Section 130, the speaker's acceptance of death has merged with his affection and faith. He believes that he will not lose his faith or his friend "though I die."

Difficulty: *Challenging*
Objective: *Essay*

20. Student answers will vary. Some students will see Tennyson as a conservative because of his tone and typical Victorian values. Others will argue that his choice of subjects and his style make him innovative. Answers should be well supported.

Difficulty: *Average*
Objective: *Essay*

"My Last Duchess," "Life in a Love," and "Porphyria's Lover" by Robert Browning
Sonnet 43 by Elizabeth Barrett Browning

Vocabulary Warm-up Exercises, p. 26

A. 1. sullen
2. baffled

3. ideal
4. ample
5. rarity
6. prevail
7. exceed
8. earnest

B. Sample Answers
1. Before giving an <u>approving</u> response to a new dish, the chef makes sure the ingredients are fresh.
2. With a nervous look on his face, the toddler <u>warily</u> accepted the cookie.
3. To <u>pursue</u> a career in sports, it is important to stay in shape.
4. I will be quiet while you're working so I won't <u>vex</u> you.
5. Shawn <u>avowed</u> his innocence, and everyone believed him.
6. I make no <u>pretense</u> to be an expert, but I know what kind of art I like.
7. By <u>trifling</u> with Janelle's feelings, you will make her unhappy.
8. To <u>spite</u> his neighbor, Hank dumped his own leaves into his neighbor's yard.

Reading Warm-up A, p. 27

Sample Answers
1. (confusing), (frustrating); I was *baffled* by the directions the policeman had given me.
2. <u>their ability to understand</u>; Another word for *exceed* is *surpass*.
3. (best); <u>to express emotions, to bring a thought to life</u>
4. <u>insincere</u>; A word that means the same as *earnest* is *sincere*.
5. <u>time and thought</u>; In comic books, good usually will *prevail* over evil.
6. <u>to find a poem that evokes a response</u>; A phrase that means the same as *rarity* is *very unusual*.
7. (negative); (happily)
8. <u>poets whose work impresses or inspires them</u>; A phrase that means the opposite of *ample* is *not enough*.

Reading Warm-up B, p. 28

Sample Answers
1. <u>their courtship</u>; Bob wished to *pursue* his desire to play in a band.
2. <u>none of his children should marry</u>; A synonym for *avowed* is *declared*.
3. <u>took her parents' feelings seriously</u>; *Trifling* in this sentence means treating their feelings lightly or ignoring them; When Jan refused to respond to his letter, Garrett felt that she was *trifling* with his affections.
4. <u>their marriage</u>; Getting stuck in a traffic jam when I am late for something might *vex* me.

5. An action designed to *spite* someone would be to intentionally embarrass them in public; A phrase that is a synonym for *spite* is *be petty*.

6. <u>a complete source of information about the history of Florence</u>; Flynn enjoys doing magic tricks, but makes no *pretense* to be a skilled magician.

7. (uncertain); A word that means the opposite of *warily* is *confidently*.

8. (smiling in recognition); Readers might find themselves having an *approving* response to Browning's poetry because it is straightforward and its themes stand the test of time.

Literary Analysis: Dramatic Monologue, p. 29

A. Sample Answers

"My Last Duchess"

Setting: sixteenth-century Italian castle; Speaker: Duke; Listener: agent for Count; Conflict: Duke hopes to marry the Count's daughter and, while negotiating with the agent, discusses his former wife.

"Life in a Love"

Setting: present day; Speaker: a spurned lover; Listener: object of speaker's affections; Conflict: The speaker pursues a woman who does not return his affections.

"Porphyria's Lover"

Setting: a cold stormy night, inside a house with a fire in the fireplace; Speaker: An unknown man; Listener: sitting with a dead woman and telling what happened—so he is either talking to himself or to someone who has come into the house; Conflict: Porphyria tells the speaker that she loves him and he is very happy, and then he kills her.

B. Sample Answers

1. run-on
2. run-on
3. run-on
4. end-stopped

Reading Strategy: Compare and Contrast Speakers in Poems, p. 30

Sample Answers

1. Speaker is jealous and possessive to the point where he kills the object of his love./ Nothing. I would not hurt someone or something I love./ My little sister. I would always protect her no matter what.

2. Speaker sees her love as everything—her whole life./ Soccer. Sometimes I feel as if it is the only thing I care about./ My family. I love them but must get away sometimes.

Vocabulary Builder, p. 31

A. 1. absence; 2. presence; 3. diligence; 4. innocence
B. 1. E; 2. A; 3. B; 4. G; 5. I; 6. D; 7. H; 8. C 9. F

Enrichment: Fine Art, p. 33

Sample Answers

Antea by Parmigianino and "My Last Duchess" Visual Details: young woman, elegantly dressed, composed and open countenance

Related Lines from Poem: "That's my last Duchess painted on the wall, / Looking as if she were alive"; "The depth and passion of its earnest glance"

Reflection of Poet's Theme: Some forms of romantic love are extremely possessive; and interest the beloved shows to other things or people incites jealousy. To desire to tamp out this interest, though, is in some sense to desire to stamp out the beloved. Owning a portrait of the beloved is a symbolic compromise: as in this painting, the liveliness and individuality of the person is present, yet they are "there" only for the viewer.

La Pia de Tolommei by Dante Gabriel Rossetti and "Porphyria's Lover"

Visual Details: grey sky, sundial, draped clothing in Renaissance style, flowing hair, pensive gaze

Related Lines from Poem: "So, she was come through wind and rain . . ./ That moment she was mine, mine fair, / Perfectly pure and good"

Reflection of the Poet's Theme: In the painting, as well as in the poem, a peaceful face, full of life, contrasts with darkness and pending violence.

Poetry of Robert Browning and Elizabeth Barrett Browning

Open-Book Test, p. 34

Short Answer

1. The introduction to the monologue explains that the Duke is addressing an agent; lines 49–51 address the listener, saying "The Count your master" and referencing the dowry for the employer's daughter. The Duke, therefore, is addressing the agent representing the father of the woman the Duke hopes to marry.
   Difficulty: *Average*   **Objective:** *Literary Analysis*

2. His family name is old and respected, and he considers it very valuable. In his view, the appreciation that his last duchess had for his name was not adequate.
   Difficulty: *Average*   **Objective:** *Interpretation*

3. The speaker addresses a silent listener.
   Difficulty: *Easy*   **Objective:** *Literary Analysis*

4. Love that is not reciprocated is a strain, but it still consumes the speaker's life.
   Difficulty: *Average*   **Objective:** *Interpretation*

5. "My life is a fault at last, I fear." The speaker feels that love is unattainable, yet he continues to seek it, allowing the quest to consume his life.
   Difficulty: *Average*   **Objective:** *Literary Analysis*

6. The turning point occurs in line 37, when the speaker says that he "found a thing to do" after it became clear that Porphyria worshiped him and was totally his.

Difficulty: *Challenging*   **Objective:** *Interpretation*

7. Students may point to such lines as 6, 8, 10, 12, 21, 23, 27, 31, 32, 33, 38, 39, or 44.

Difficulty: *Easy*   **Objective:** *Literary Analysis*

8. Students should recognize that both speakers are egotistical, possessive, arrogant, and violent. However, the Duke in "My Last Duchess" merely implies his complicity in his last duchess's death, while Porphyria's lover openly admits that he strangled her. In addition, the Duke in "My Last Duchess" is socially snobbish, a trait that is not evident in Porphyria's lover.

Difficulty: *Challenging*   **Objective:** *Reading*

9. Sample answer: The comparison of the innumerable ways of loving suggests that the love is boundless.

Difficulty: *Average*   **Objective:** *Interpretation*

10. He or she could be described as generous to a lavish degree.

Difficulty: *Average*   **Objective:** *Vocabulary*

Essay

11. Students' essays should show an understanding of the Duke's jealousy, snobbishness, and possessiveness. They should cite the Duke's attitude that his noble, ancient name deserves the Duchess's full attention and devotion.

Difficulty: *Easy*   **Objective:** *Essay*

12. Some students may consider that the speaker in "My Last Duchess" reveals the most because the Duke, intent on winning over the Count's agent, probably alienates him with what he says about his dead wife. In saying that his wife had "A heart—how shall I say?—too soon made glad," the Duke reveals that his own heart is cold and hardened.

Difficulty: *Average*   **Objective:** *Essay*

13. Students' essays should address the central messages or themes of the two poems selected. Then, students should support their thesis with examples of comparisons and contrasts in the poems.

Difficulty: *Challenging*   **Objective:** *Essay*

14. Students' essays should note Browning's unconventional choice of subjects—for example, the juxtaposition of marriage or love with violence in works like "My Last Duchess" and "Porphyria's Lover," or the characterization of the speakers in these two dramatic monologues as monomaniacal and obsessive. Students should also point to one or more of the following elements: verse form, dramatic monologue, diction, and characterization.

Difficulty: *Average*   **Objective:** *Essay*

Oral Response

15. Oral responses should be clear, well organized, and well supported by appropriate details from the selections.

Difficulty: *Average*   **Objective:** *Oral Interpretation*

Selection Test A, p. 37

Critical Reading

1. ANS: C	DIF: Easy	OBJ: Comprehension
2. ANS: A	DIF: Easy	OBJ: Comprehension
3. ANS: A	DIF: Easy	OBJ: Reading Strategy
4. ANS: D	DIF: Easy	OBJ: Literary Analysis
5. ANS: C	DIF: Easy	OBJ: Interpretation
6. ANS: B	DIF: Easy	OBJ: Reading Strategy
7. ANS: D	DIF: Easy	OBJ: Comprehension
8. ANS: B	DIF: Easy	OBJ: Comprehension
9. ANS: A	DIF: Easy	OBJ: Reading Strategy
10. ANS: C	DIF: Easy	OBJ: Interpretation
11. ANS: B	DIF: Easy	OBJ: Comprehension

Vocabulary and Grammar

12. ANS: C	DIF: Easy	OBJ: Vocabulary
13. ANS: A	DIF: Easy	OBJ: Vocabulary
14. ANS: D	DIF: Easy	OBJ: Grammar

Essay

15. Students should recognize that although the two poems both discuss romantic love, the love relationship described in "Life in a Love" is not as deep as the one described in Sonnet 43. In "Life in a Love," the speaker is pursuing a woman whom he loves. She continually rejects him, he becomes discouraged, but then a look from her renews his confidence and he pursues her once more. Sonnet 43 is about an intense and fully grown love that involves the speaker's entire being.

Difficulty: *Easy*

Objective: *Essay*

16. Students should note that the speaker is mentally unstable and dangerous. This information comes from the speaker, who states that he is happy that Porphyria loves him and then kills her. The reader still has the following questions: Does the speaker know he committed a murder? Does the speaker have a reason for doing what he did?

Difficulty: *Easy*

Objective: *Essay*

17. Students should discuss Browning's unconventional characterization of love with violence in works like "My

Last Duchess" and "Porphyria's Lover." They should also discuss the obsessive, violent characters of the speakers.

Difficulty: *Average*
Objective: *Essay*

Selection Test B, p. 40

Critical Reading

1. ANS: C	DIF: Easy	OBJ: Comprehension
2. ANS: D	DIF: Average	OBJ: Reading Strategy
3. ANS: A	DIF: Average	OBJ: Literary Analysis
4. ANS: B	DIF: Easy	OBJ: Literary Analysis
5. ANS: D	DIF: Average	OBJ: Reading Strategy
6. ANS: D	DIF: Easy	OBJ: Comprehension
7. ANS: B	DIF: Average	OBJ: Interpretation
8. ANS: B	DIF: Challenging	OBJ: Interpretation
9. ANS: C	DIF: Average	OBJ: Literary Analysis
10. ANS: C	DIF: Average	OBJ: Comprehension
11. ANS: B	DIF: Challenging	OBJ: Reading Strategy
12. ANS: D	DIF: Average	OBJ: Interpretation

Vocabulary and Grammar

13. ANS: D	DIF: Average	OBJ: Vocabulary
14. ANS: C	DIF: Easy	OBJ: Vocabulary
15. ANS: B	DIF: Average	OBJ: Vocabulary
16. ANS: C	DIF: Average	OBJ: Grammar
17. ANS: C	DIF: Average	OBJ: Grammar

Essay

18. Students should recognize that all three of Robert Browning's poems are dramatic monologues; they each feature a single character who reveals his personality through his words to a silent listener. For example, students might note that the speaker in "My Last Duchess" directly reveals his pride by boasting about the painting to the Count's agent. Indirectly, the speaker also reveals his arrogance, jealousy, and temper with his remarks about his deceased wife.

Difficulty: *Easy*
Objective: *Essay*

19. Some students may contend that the speaker in "My Last Duchess" reveals the most because the Duke, intent on winning over the Count's agent, probably alienates him with what he says about his dead wife. In saying that his wife had "A heart—how shall I say?—too soon made glad," the Duke reveals that his own heart is cold and hardened.

Difficulty: *Average*
Objective: *Essay*

20. Students' answers should note Browning's unconventional choice of subjects—for example, the juxtaposition of marriage and violence in "My Last Duchess" and "Porphyria's Lover" or the characterization of the speakers

in these two dramatic monologues as monomaniacal and obsessive. Students should also point to one or more of the following elements: verse form, monologue, diction, and characterization.

Difficulty: *Average*
Objective: *Essay*

from **Hard Times** by Charles Dickens

Vocabulary Warm-up Exercises, p. 44

A. 1. reign
2. contradiction
3. discard
4. established
5. immense
6. dismal
7. feeble
8. maim

B. Sample Answers

1. False. People who have the <u>conviction</u> that they're always right do not engage in give and take.
2. False. A <u>nonsensical</u> answer is one that makes no sense, so would not be appreciated by a teacher.
3. False. If a book is <u>objectionable</u> to parents, schools will hesitate to use it.
4. True. An opinion that is <u>inflexible</u> is rigid.
5. True. <u>Lustrous</u> means shiny, so the sun would enhance this quality.
6. False. Sports are <u>regulated</u> to make games fair for all teams.
7. True. The word <u>ventured</u> implies that risk is involved.
8. True. <u>Representations</u> are likenesses.

Reading Warm-up A, p. 45

Sample Answers

1. (Queen Victoria); *Reign* usually implies royalty, while *term* means the period of time that an elected leader is in office.
2. (bleak); An antonym for *dismal* is *cheerful.*
3. <u>what were known as the three Rs: reading, writing, and arithmetic</u>; Karl's parents always *emphasized* good manners at the table.
4. (disagreed); Another word for *contradiction* is *opposition.*
5. <u>beaten hard</u>; *Injure* is a synonym for *maim.*
6. (expense); *Immense* clouds of smoke rose from the burning cornfield.
7. <u>their assignments</u>; An antonym for *discard* is *retain.*
8. (girls); *Weak* is a synonym for *feeble.*

Reading Warm-up B, p. 46

Sample Answers

1. (ridiculous); I can't get that *nonsensical* nursery rhyme out of my head.

2. the real people Dickens knew; In his work there were also *representations* of factory life.

3. The words "violence" and "cruelty" give clues that *objectionable* means something that might bother people. Today people know what is *objectionable* in the movies from reviews and ratings.

4. (glowing); A word that means the opposite of *lustrous* is *dull.*

5. grimy and dangerous parts of London; We *ventured* to the edge of the cliff to see the view.

6. (rigid); The rule that weapons are not allowed on airplanes is *inflexible.*

7. working conditions should be regulated to protect children; A *conviction* is a firm belief, while an *idea* can be changed easily.

8. Dickens thought working conditions for children should be *regulated.* I agree with this because children are not able to speak up for their own rights.

Dickens Biography, p. 47

Sample Answers

1. I cannot believe it! My father has been sent to debtor's prison and I am on my own. I work in a factory all day. Hours on end without anything to eat. The boss walks by and glares at me. I work seven days a week. I cannot attend school anymore. I miss the reading and writing the most. I long to write as I paste labels all day long!

2. It is only nine months since *The Pickwick Papers* was published, but boy, how my life has changed! I believe I am famous. I have been asked for my autograph many times now. Me, a boy who used to live on the streets! I am surprised and relieved to have such a success. I hope this is just the first of many more successes.

3. I have just woken up from a nightmare, which is always the same. My wife shakes me gently and offers me a glass of water. I look at her as though she were a stranger. It takes me a while to figure out that I am a grown man and that she is the woman who bore me ten children. I am no longer that poor, abandoned boy.

Literary Analysis: The Novel and Social Criticism, p. 48

1. He does not like Gradgrind's aggressive teaching style, which destroys all imagination and wonder and fills students' heads with only facts. He is criticizing the way in which the school is run.

2. He refers to her in this way because he thinks of students as parts of a system, not as individuals. Dickens is critical of this approach to education.

3. He is criticizing the nonsensical and useless nature of the facts the students have to memorize and recite.

4. Dickens feels that teachers lack individuality and that they are taught the same way as the students, as though they were all the same. The reference to a "factory" makes them a product rather than individuals.

Reading Strategy: Recognize the Writer's Purpose, p. 49

Sample Answers

1. The schoolroom is described as being a "plain, bare, monotonous vault." The speaker is described as having a "wide, thin, hard set" mouth; an "inflexible, dry, and dictatorial" voice; bristling hair; and a square, boxy figure. The author sees the schoolroom as a boring, rigid, unwelcoming place.

2. Sissy is shy and unable to fit into the rigid classroom. Bitzer is responsive and precise; he is able to give the teachers exactly what they want. In the sunlight, Sissy appears natural and glowing, while Bitzer appears drained of all color. Sissy's clash with her teachers reinforces the author's negative view of the classroom and its teachers. The author does not approve of the teachers' rigid teaching styles, not of the way they ban imagination and individuality from their classroom.

3. Students should select a paragraph and rewrite it with positive details that would change the tone of the story from one in which the educational system is being criticized to one in which it is being praised. For example, the physical appearance of the classroom can be described as light and airy and bright, etc.

Vocabulary Builder, p. 50

A. 1. monolithic
2. monogram
3. monophony
4. monosyllabic

B. 1. D; 2. C; 3. A; 4. B; 5. C; 6. C; 7. A; 8. B

Grammar and Style: Avoiding Shifts in Verb Tense, p. 51

A. 1. Sissy learned that Mr. Gradgrind liked only facts and did not appreciate original thought.

2. The students in the class will grow up and understand that Mr. Gradgrind was wrong about his philosophy on education and they will lose respect for him.

3. Bitzer appreciates the discussion on horses because it is amusing and it distracts the class from the math homework.

B. Sample Answers

Students should learn to think and reason. Students who are taught only facts grow up to be like robots. The students who are taught to think and reason will be creative, productive members of society. Students who come out of a classroom like the one in the Dickens story (will have learned) nothing that will benefit society."

Enrichment: Philosophy, p. 53

Sample Answers

1. Promoting the common good is a good goal. One example is environmentalism. If we all work to do the right thing for the environment, everyone benefits.

2. Gradgrind is shown to be only a rigid teacher of facts. He tells students they must clear their minds of anything that does not have a useful application in society. Dickens reveals his negative attitude toward this philosophy in his unflattering portrayal of the teacher.

3. One negative part of the philosophy is that individuality and creativity are stifled. If people are forced into certain professions for the common good, they cannot pursue their own individual goals and dreams.

from Hard Times by Charles Dickens

Open-Book Test, p. 54

Short Answer

1. Dickens focuses on the social issue of education.
   Difficulty: *Easy*   **Objective:** *Interpretation*

2. Students' charts may include the following types of responses: ideas—education, teaching, fact-based teaching and learning; choice of characters' names—Gradgrind, Sissy Jupe, Bitzer, M'Choakumchild; attitudes toward characters—disgust, sarcasm, scorn, absurdity; outcome—Sissy Jupe is humiliated, Gradgrind and the third gentleman can't get past the facts, and M'Choakumchild knows too much to teach. Dickens is pointing out the absurdity and impracticality of teaching only facts without supplying context.
   Difficulty: *Average*   **Objective:** *Reading*

3. Gradgrind has a hard-nosed, unforgiving approach; he wants to elicit facts at whatever cost to understanding. Students' examples may be drawn from any of the interactions that Gradgrind has with Sissy Jupe or Bitzer.
   Difficulty: *Average*   **Objective:** *Interpretation*

4. The focus of the teaching portrayed in the excerpt is completely on facts; no allowance is made for creativity or for understanding the applications of the facts.
   Difficulty: *Challenging*   **Objective:** *Interpretation*

5. An *adversary* is an opponent or an enemy. In the final paragraph, the adversary is M'Choakumchild.
   Difficulty: *Average*   **Objective:** *Vocabulary*

6. He thinks nicknames are silly and not to be used.
   Difficulty: *Easy*   **Objective:** *Interpretation*

7. Dickens wants readers to know that teachers were all educated in exactly the same way with no allowance for creativity or individuality.
   Difficulty: *Easy*   **Objective:** *Interpretation*

8. Dickens's target is a system of education that treats children like machines.
   Difficulty: *Easy*   **Objective:** *Literary Analysis*

9. Dickens wants to criticize the fact that students in the overpopulated school are treated as numbers, not as individuals.
   Difficulty: *Average*   **Objective:** *Literary Analysis*

10. Dickens's tone could be described as ironic, critical, or indignant.
    Difficulty: *Average*   **Objective:** *Interpretation*

Essay

11. Diary entries should focus on Mr. Gradgrind's teaching methods and on the student-writer's own experiences in class. Students should write their entries with a consistent first-person point of view.
    Difficulty: *Easy*   **Objective:** *Essay*

12. Students should note that Sissy Jupe is a quiet girl who has not yet learned to conform to the rigid ideas of her classroom. Bitzer, on the other hand, is an eager student who promptly tells the teacher what he wants to hear. He gives a complete definition of the horse, for example, sticking only to the facts. Lacking in his definition, however, are any details or images relating to the beauty of a horse. Dickens focuses on these characters to show a contrast between people caught up in facts and people who still possess imagination and innocence.
    Difficulty: *Average*   **Objective:** *Essay*

13. Students may note in their essays that the indirect criticism that Dickens voices within the framework of a fictional narrative has the advantage of an entertaining appeal, as well as the use of sharp irony. Dickens's use of fiction for social criticism may well have had more persuasive impact than if he had chosen a nonfiction format to express his ideas. Evaluate students' essays on clarity, coherence, and specific support.
    Difficulty: *Challenging*   **Objective:** *Essay*

14. Students' responses will vary. Some will maintain that the excerpt supports the view that Dickens both hoped for and expected substantial reforms. Other students may argue that the satirical tone of the novel excerpt is predominantly negative, and that Dickens fails to put forward a positive alternative. Evaluate students' writing on clarity, coherence, and specific support.
    Difficulty: *Average*   **Objective:** *Essay*

Oral Response

15. Oral responses should be clear, well organized, and well supported by appropriate details from the selection.
    Difficulty: *Average*   **Objective:** *Oral Interpretation*

Selection Test A, p. 57

Critical Reading

1. ANS: A   DIF: Easy   OBJ: Comprehension
2. ANS: C   DIF: Easy   OBJ: Comprehension
3. ANS: B   DIF: Easy   OBJ: Interpretation
4. ANS: D   DIF: Easy   OBJ: Interpretation
5. ANS: C   DIF: Easy   OBJ: Reading Strategy
6. ANS: D   DIF: Easy   OBJ: Literary Analysis
7. ANS: B   DIF: Easy   OBJ: Literary Analysis
8. ANS: A   DIF: Easy   OBJ: Interpretation
9. ANS: C   DIF: Easy   OBJ: Reading Strategy
10. ANS: B   DIF: Easy   OBJ: Interpretation
11. ANS: D   DIF: Easy   OBJ: Interpretation

Vocabulary and Grammar

12. ANS: D   DIF: Easy   OBJ: Vocabulary
13. ANS: B   DIF: Easy   OBJ: Vocabulary
14. ANS: C   DIF: Easy   OBJ: Grammar

Essay

15. Student answers will vary. Students should be evaluated of their ability to allude to the problem they wish to address, without actually stating it outright. Student essays should imitate the style of exaggeration found in the selection.
    Difficulty: *Easy*
    Objective: *Essay*
16. Student answers will vary. Students should be evaluated on the clarity and coherence of the journal entry, and their use of supporting detail should they choose to represent one of Dickens's characters.
    Difficulty: *Easy*
    Objective: *Essay*
17. Students' responses will vary. Some will maintain that the excerpt supports the view that Dickens both hoped for and expected substantial reforms. Other students may argue that the satirical tone of the novel excerpt is predominantly negative, and that Dickens fails to put forward a positive alternative. Evaluate students' writing on clarity, coherence, and specific support.
    Difficulty: *Average*
    Objective: *Essay*

Selection Test B, p. 60

Critical Reading

1. ANS: C   DIF: Easy   OBJ: Comprehension
2. ANS: A   DIF: Average   OBJ: Reading Strategy
3. ANS: C   DIF: Easy   OBJ: Comprehension
4. ANS: B   DIF: Average   OBJ: Literary Analysis
5. ANS: D   DIF: Average   OBJ: Reading Strategy
6. ANS: C   DIF: Easy   OBJ: Interpretation
7. ANS: B   DIF: Challenging   OBJ: Literary Analysis
8. ANS: B   DIF: Average   OBJ: Reading Strategy
9. ANS: A   DIF: Easy   OBJ: Comprehension
10. ANS: B   DIF: Average   OBJ: Reading Strategy
11. ANS: B   DIF: Average   OBJ: Reading Strategy
12. ANS: C   DIF: Average   OBJ: Literary Analysis
13. ANS: A   DIF: Average   OBJ: Literary Analysis
14. ANS: C   DIF: Average   OBJ: Interpretation

Vocabulary and Grammar

15. ANS: D   DIF: Easy   OBJ: Grammar
16. ANS: C   DIF: Average   OBJ: Grammar
17. ANS: A   DIF: Average   OBJ: Vocabulary

Essay

18. Student answers will vary but they should address the factual emphasis of the education in *Hard Times* as well as the expectation that students all conform and be the same and the resistance to using imagination or "fancy." Students should compare this to the education they have received and tell to what extent it is similar and different.
    Difficulty: *Average*
    Objective: *Essay*
19. Student responses will vary. Some students will argue that the excerpt supports the view that Dickens both hoped for and expected substantial reforms. Other students may argue that the satirical tone of the novel excerpt is predominately negative, and that Dickens fails to put forth a positive alternative.
    Difficulty: *Average*
    Objective: *Essay*

from Hard Times by Charles Dickens
from Upheaval by Anton Chekov

Literary Analysis: Social Criticism, p. 63

Dickens

1. ineffective schooling that focuses on memorizing facts/ "Teach these boys and girls nothing but facts"/exaggeration and dystopia/characters believe their system is good; Sissy feels that something is wrong.
2. education system drains the life out of students/the description of Bitzer's colorless face/exaggeration/ characters are unaware

Chekhov

1. the disparity of the classes and the ill treatment that comes with it/"the feeling that is so familiar to persons

in dependent positions, who eat the bread of the rich and powerful and cannot speak their minds."/realism/ Yes, character's thoughts are directly critical of society's ills.

2. powerlessness of the poor/"They could do what they liked with her"/realism/Yes, the character is aware of the issue.

Vocabulary Builder, p. 64

A. Possible Responses
1. kindred
2. rummaging
3. palpitations
4. ingratiating
5. turmoil

B. 1. C; 2. D; 3. A; 4. E; 5. B

Support for Writing, p. 65

Sample Answers

1. *Hard Times*: School system drains creativity and individuality out of students.

   Upheaval: the disparity between classes and the resulting uneven distribution of power

2. *Hard Times*: classroom has some realistic aspects: teacher/student relationship, etc.

   Upheaval: Realistic setting—realistic main character and situation

3. *Hard Times*: exaggerations—teacher is over the top in his insistence on facts; students are described as caricatures. It is a dystopia.

   Upheaval: maybe slight exaggeration in the obliviousness of the rich woman but plausible enough to be real

4. Students should give opinions about which is more effective—for example: *Upheaval* convinced me that a problem existed that needed to be solved because the realistic aspects show problems that are really present in society, whereas in *Hard Times* the situation is so extreme that it seems as though it can't possibly be that bad.

"*from* Jane Eyre" by Charlotte Brontë

Vocabulary Warm-up Exercise A, p. 69

A. 1. gleeful
2. punctual
3. merit
4. commendations
5. crevices
6. retained
7. ominous
8. abyss

B. Sample Answers
1. a - inactive
2. b - forethought

3. c - achieved
4. a - liveliness
5. b - limit
6. a - pondering
7. a - obtained
8. c - distribute

Reading Warm-up A, p. 70

Sample Answers

1. (vast)(empty); When there are few options, the future can seem like an <u>abyss</u>.
2. <u>high point</u>; An antonym for *gleeful* is *miserable*.
3. <u>the attic's unfinished walls</u>; Another word for *crevices* is *cracks*.
4. (disapprove); An action that might receive *commendations* is rescuing someone from a fire.
5. <u>needlework or piano practice</u>; *Value* is a synonym for *merit*.
6. (creaking); Jack's face wore an *ominous* expression before he broke the news.
7. <u>her composure</u>; An antonym for *retained* is *released*.
8. (time); *Late* is an antonym for *punctual*.

Reading Warm-up B, p. 71

Sample Answers

1. (reserved); A word that means the opposite of *passive* is *active*.
2. <u>modesty</u>; Although usually noisy, Libby showed *restraint* in the library.
3. (strong feelings); A synonym for *vitality* is *liveliness*.
4. (advice); *Dispense* is to give something out, while *share* usually means to keep part for oneself.
5. <u>the same social status as men</u>; After years of training, Josh *attained* his black belt.
6. (prediction); No, I don't agree with their decision, because usually parents buy books, not children.
7. <u>pleasure from following Harry's adventurers</u>; A synonym for *derived* is *drew*.
8. (think); Glen wore a *pensive* look on his face as he considered the problem.

from Jane Eyre by Charlotte Brontë

Literary Analysis: Author's Political and Philosophical Assumptions, p. 72

Sample Answers

1. Sewing is a normal part of a girl's education at school.
2. Teachers are permitted to verbally abuse and whip their students.
3. To be truly good, one must employ great discipline and suffering.
4. Reader knows who Felix is; reader reads the Bible.

Reading Strategy: Analyze an Author's Assumptions, p. 73

Sample Answers

1. assumption: It is OK for a teacher to abuse students.

   Brontë's position: She was against this abuse and thought it should change.

2. assumption: People should not be abused or treated poorly no matter what/People—including children at school—are entitled to individual rights.

   Brontë's position: She is in favor of this.

3. assumption: Students like Helen have their spirit broken and are sad.

   Brontë's position: This is bad for the student. The educational system must be reformed.

4. assumption: People must bear up to what they must endure. In this case, students must put up with abuse.

   Brontë's position: Brontë feels that putting up with this kind of abuse would just allow this bad system to continue. . . she feels people must speak up for change.

Vocabulary Builder, p. 74

Sample Answers

A. 1. The man's thinness was obscured by his baggy clothing, so I had no idea how thin he really was.

2. The grocery list comprised only sweets.

3. It was not unusual to come into my sister's room and find sundry items on her floor, all of which belonged to me.

4. Bringing the new puppy into my house caused a tumult, with my other dog barking and my children running around.

5. Jane Eyre could be considered truculent when compared to the standard behavior of girls at the time.

B. 6. A; 7. D; 8. D

Support for Writing, p. 75

Sample Answers:

Helen Burns

schoolwork: she drifts off a lot; can't pay attention
effort: bad attitude; pays attention only when she likes material; daydreams
personal hygiene: didn't wash under her nails; slovenly habits
posture: standing on the side of her shoe; poking out her chin; head droops

Ms Scatcherd

"Burns, you are standing on the side of your shoe. . ."/very critical, picks on every minor, unimportant thing.

"You dirty, disagreeable girl."/insults students in abusive way

Whips Burns/thinks physical abuse is OK. Violent.

Enrichment: Film Production of *Jane Eyre*, p. 76

Sample Answers

Summary: Helen is abused by her teacher and puts up with it. Jane thinks that the teacher is not acting properly and that Helen is being mistreated.

Issues: How should kids be treated by adults in their lives?

Modern-day comparison: A kid is being abused by his parent. A friend tells him not to stand for the abuse.

Idea: Jane & Helen are friends. Helen is being physically hit by her father. Jane helps her see that it is not okay and that she should get help.

from Jane Eyre, by Charlotte Bronte

Open-Book Test, p. 77

Short Answer

1. Jane wants to find out what Helen feels about school at Lowood. She has observed the harsh treatment Helen has received from Miss Scatcherd, and she wants to know why Helen does not rebel against the way she is treated.

   Difficulty: *Average*   **Objective:** *Interpretation*

2. Jane feels she should never have to tolerate cruel or unjust treatment, even from a teacher. Helen, by contrast, feels that she must endure severity in order to overcome her faults. Evaluations of persuasive arguments will vary.

   Difficulty: *Challenging*   **Objective:** *Interpretation*

3. The word *obscure* in this context means "not readily seen." Miss Scatcherd keeps calling on and addressing Helen Burns, making it impossible for the girl to go unnoticed.

   Difficulty: *Average*   **Objective:** *Vocabulary*

4. Students' responses should be a paraphrase of Helen's explanation that " . . . Miss Temple has generally something to say which is newer to me than my own reflections: her language is singularly agreeable to me, and the information she communicates is often just what I wished to know."

   Difficulty: *Average*   **Objective:** *Interpretation*

5. She wants the reader to know the discomforts at Lowood.

   Difficulty: *Easy*   **Objective:** *Reading*

6. Helen says that Miss Scatcherd treats her harshly because Helen has faults that need correcting. The explanation suggests that Helen is trying to find some logical explanation for the treatment. Helen is also modest.

   Difficulty: *Challenging*   **Objective:** *Interpretation*

7. Helen Burns might be described as dutiful, patient, and self-aware.

   Difficulty: *Average*   **Objective:** *Interpretation*

8. Lowood believes students should be accepting, patient, and aware that they have faults.

   Difficulty: *Average*   **Objective:** *Interpretation*

9. Sample answer: The first-person point of view makes the events and characters seem more realistic, vivid, and immediate.

   Difficulty: *Challenging*   **Objective:** *Interpretation*

10. Sample answer: Brontë's novel condemns the educational practices of a Victorian boarding school. The classroom situation at this type of school is depicted, discussed, analyzed, and found lacking.

    Difficulty: *Easy*   **Objective:** *Literary Analysis*

Essay

11. Students should recognize that both Jane and Helen are good people who wish to be kind and as good as their human natures permit. Jane, however, is more rebellious and wishes to respond in kind to the injustice and cruelty of others. She believes that only by so doing will others learn to treat her with respect. Helen, on the other hand, believes that holding such anger and ill feeling toward others causes unhappiness and does not really achieve anything in the end.

    Difficulty: *Easy*   **Objective:** *Essay*

12. Students' responses will vary. Evaluate students' letters on clarity, coherence, inventiveness, and consistency with Charlotte Brontë's characterizations in the selection.

    Difficulty: *Average*   **Objective:** *Essay*

13. Students' essays should address the harsh, unrelenting style of Miss Scatcherd and the positive, encouraging approach of Miss Temple. Students should also explain that Helen feels that she needs to be reminded of her faults so that she can correct them. Students' opinions about the better teaching style should be supported.

    Difficulty: *Challenging*   **Objective:** *Essay*

14. Responses will vary, although in general students should note that Helen seems more a product or reflection of her society, while Jane seems more eager to exert an active influence on social trends, at least in education and the rearing of children. Evaluate students' writing on clarity, coherence, and specific support.

    Difficulty: *Average*   **Objective:** *Essay*

Oral Response

15. Oral responses should be clear, well organized, and well supported by appropriate details from the selection.

    Difficulty: *Average*   **Objective:** *Oral Interpretation*

Selection Test A, p. 80

Critical Reading

1. **ANS:** C   **DIF:** Easy   **OBJ:** Comprehension
2. **ANS:** A   **DIF:** Easy   **OBJ:** Comprehension

3. **ANS:** C   **DIF:** Easy   **OBJ:** Comprehension
4. **ANS:** B   **DIF:** Easy   **OBJ:** Literary Analysis
5. **ANS:** A   **DIF:** Easy   **OBJ:** Literary Analysis
6. **ANS:** C   **DIF:** Easy   **OBJ:** Literary Analysis
7. **ANS:** A   **DIF:** Easy   **OBJ:** Reading Strategy
8. **ANS:** D   **DIF:** Easy   **OBJ:** Reading Strategy
9. **ANS:** B   **DIF:** Easy   **OBJ:** Interpretation
10. **ANS:** D   **DIF:** Easy   **OBJ:** Interpretation
11. **ANS:** A   **DIF:** Easy   **OBJ:** Interpretation

Vocabulary and Grammar

12. **ANS:** B   **DIF:** Easy   **OBJ:** Vocabulary
13. **ANS:** B   **DIF:** Easy   **OBJ:** Vocabulary
14. **ANS:** C   **DIF:** Easy   **OBJ:** Vocabulary

Essay

15. Students should recognize that Jane and Helen are both good people who wish to be as kind and good as their human natures permit. Jane, however, is more rebellious and wishes to respond in kind to the injustice and cruelty of others. She believes that only by doing so will others learn to treat her with respect. Helen, on the other hand, believes that holding such anger and ill feeling toward others causes unhappiness and does not really achieve anything in the end.

    Difficulty: *Easy*

    Objective: *Essay*

16. Answers will vary but may include the following: Brontë felt that the teachers did not treat students with respect and compassion. This is demonstrated by how Ms. Scatcherd treated Helen. She also felt that students learn better when they are treated better and when materials are more interesting. This is demonstrated by the example of Miss Miller. Helen saw herself as a "bad" person because she wasn't able to focus all the time, so expectations must have been to focus all the time and be perfectly behaved. Brontë feels these are unrealistic expectations.

    Difficulty: *Easy*

    Objective: *Essay*

17. Answers will vary. Students should select a social trend and discuss what it means to fully accept it, to reject it, or to be somewhere in between. For example—increased communication on the Internet. To reject it may mean being left out of many important and interesting things and missing out on idea exchange. On the other hand, to fully accept it may mean isolation, not developing social skills. Middle ground might be to limit computer time and make sure to balance it with social time.

    Difficulty: *Average*

    Objective: *Essay*

Selection Test B, p. 83

Critical Reading

1. ANS: B	DIF: Easy	OBJ: Comprehension
2. ANS: D	DIF: Average	OBJ: Interpretation
3. ANS: A	DIF: Challenging	OBJ: Reading Strategy
4. ANS: A	DIF: Average	OBJ: Interpretation
5. ANS: C	DIF: Easy	OBJ: Comprehension
6. ANS: C	DIF: Average	OBJ: Interpretation
7. ANS: D	DIF: Average	OBJ: Reading Strategy
8. ANS: C	DIF: Challenging	OBJ: Literary Analysis
9. ANS: B	DIF: Challenging	OBJ: Literary Analysis
10. ANS: B	DIF: Average	OBJ: Reading Strategy
11. ANS: B	DIF: Average	OBJ: Reading Strategy
12. ANS: B	DIF: Average	OBJ: Interpretation
13. ANS: A	DIF: Easy	OBJ: Literary Analysis
14. ANS: B	DIF: Challenging	OBJ: Literary Analysis

Vocabulary and Grammar

15. ANS: A	DIF: Average	OBJ: Vocabulary
16. ANS: D	DIF: Average	OBJ: Vocabulary
17. ANS: B	DIF: Average	OBJ: Vocabulary

Essay

18. Students should say that Helen and Jane discuss their lives at Lowood. The conversation reveals that Helen is humble, passive, and critical of herself. Any troubles that she encounters at the school, she blames on herself. She also forces herself to forgive people who are cruel to her. Jane, on the other hand, is much more inclined to fight back and defend her rights. Helen's philosophy of life is that one's tone must be passive, understanding and forgiving. Jane is not forgiving and lives in the present.

    Difficulty: *Average*

    Objective: *Essay*

19. Student responses will vary. Evaluate students' letters on clarity, coherence, inventiveness, and consistency with Bronte's characters in the selection.

20. Responses will vary. Students should note that Helen seems more a product or reflection of her society, while Jane seems more eager to exert an active influence on social trends, at least in education and the rearing of children. Evaluate student writing on clarity, coherence, and specific support.

    Difficulty: *Average*

    Objective: *Essay*

From the Author's Desk

James Berry Introduces "From Lucy: Englan' Lady," "Time Removed," and "Freedom," p. 86

1. Berry had a Jamaican upbringing, a British identity, and an African background.

2. Kipling's poem foresees some of the dangers of power and pomp in the British empire.

3. Lucy treats the Queen like an ancient institution, worthy of reverence; at the same time, she considers the Queen as someone close to her and very human, for whom she feels sympathy. Lucy's outlook represents the uncritical admiration that many ordinary people feel for royalty.

4. He felt saddened by how little had happened during his absence.

5. In England, there was a sense of a landscape managed through the application of knowledge and skill. In Jamaica, the landscape and roads were still undeveloped.

6. He explains the title by saying that, although he was removed from the time of his childhood, he still felt part of it in a helpless way.

7. Berry believes that people must free themselves from their own pain and past. Righteous indignation, he says, is unproductive. Caribbean people must embark on a renaissance, letting go of the past and creating new structures. Students' evaluations of Berry's outlook will vary. Encourage students to support their views with reasons and examples.

James Berry

Listening and Viewing, p. 87

Sample answers/guidelines

Segment 1: He was interested and curious about water, sunlight, and what made human beings individuals, as well as the environment and animals that surrounded him. These were the topics he explored in his writing. Students will discuss particular interests that they have pursued as writing topics either to learn more about the topic or to explore it and make others think about it.

Segment 2: James Berry's fascination with Caribbean speech and the female voice, based on his mother's tone, inspired him to write the poem "Lucy." Students may suggest that Berry's reading of the poem shows the natural rhythm of Caribbean speech and makes the poem seem more realistic.

Segment 3: James Berry gives his characters names; determines their physical attributes and personal details; and, if they are based on real people, distorts certain qualities in order to make them unidentifiable.

Students may suggest that they would rather completely invent a character because it is more fun and creative or that they would rather base it on someone real because that could allow them to develop the character more easily.

Segment 4: Berry means that readers can learn more about other peoples' experiences, cultures, and ways of life by reading different types of literature.

Students may suggest that reading and writing can help them identify which personal stories are most important to them and define who they are as a person. Writing allows them to share those experiences with others.

"Dover Beach" by Matthew Arnold
"Recessional" and "The Widow at Windsor"
by Rudyard Kipling

Vocabulary Warm-up Exercises, p. 89

A. 1. widow
2. vast
3. furled
4. tide
5. fling
6. valiant
7. ebb
8. retreating

B. Sample Answers

1. T; *Grating* means "making a harsh, grinding sound," which describes the sound of a chain rubbing against a metal bar.
2. T; *Lest* means "for fear that." You should wear a helmet to protect your head for fear that you might fall.
3. F; *Tremulous* means "trembling; shaking." A calm person would not be trembling.
4. F; *Glimmering* means "giving a faint, flickering light." Bright summer sunshine is not faint or flickering.
5. T; *Frantic* means "wild with anger or worry," which describes how someone running to catch a plane might feel.
6. T; *Blanched* means "pale," which is how someone who is about to faint might look.
7. T; *Certitude* means "sureness." It is good to feel sure about a decision one has made.
8. F; *Tumult* means "noise and confusion," which is the opposite of peaceful.

Reading Warm-up A, p. 90

Sample Answers

1. often sailing for several days across the great ocean; A synonym for *vast* is "large."
2. tightly; to prevent them from blowing away; *Furled* means "rolled up tightly."

3. as an angry child would throw a toy; Please don't *fling* your dirty clothes on the floor.
4. mourned a husband who had died on the job; A *widow* is a woman whose husband has died.
5. (brave); An antonym for *valiant* is *cowardly*.
6. powerful incoming . . . which could knock them down and even turn over the lifeboats; *Tide* refers to the rise and fall of ocean waters each day.
7. safety further inland; The defeated army was *retreating* to safety.
8. ocean waters after the storm had passed; *Ebb* means "lessening or decline."

Reading Warm-up B, p. 91
Sample Answers

1. dangers of shipwrecks, pirates, and attacks by enemy navies; *Certitude* means "sureness."
2. You could replace the word *lest* with "for fear that."
3. (clanging) (banging) (crashing); A synonym for *tumult* is *noise*.
4. moving metal parts in the ship's engine; Fingernails scraped against a chalkboard would make a *grating* sound.
5. (candle); A synonym for *glimmering* is *flickering* or *faint*.
6. seasickness and lack of sleep; *Blanched* means "pale."
7. fear that he could barely hold a cup of tea without spilling it; *Tremulous* means "shaking."
8. felt like a prisoner; A synonym for *frantic* is *desperate*.

Literary Analysis: Mood as a Key to Theme, p. 92

Sample Answers

1. The rhythm of the passage's image—"Begin, and cease, and then again begin,"—is calming. The poet seems to want to establish an everyday image into which sadness enters so readers understand that the sadness is "here."
2. Navies "melt away" is a sobering euphemism for soldiers being killed in battle. The allusions to Nineveh and Tyre are bold and alarming. The poet almost threatens that *this* nation could pass into obscurity, as did those cities of old.

Reading Strategy: Relate Mood and Theme to Historical Period, p. 93

Sample Answers

1. The sea of faith . . . and naked shingles of the world
2. Turbid ebb and flow of human misery
3. The Eternal note of sadness in; Turbid ebb and flow of human misery
4. lest we forget
5.
6. lord of our far-flung battle line; our navies melt away

7. Creation

8. gold crown; poor beggars goods in 'er shop; for 'alf 'o Creation she owns

9. troops, wars; pays us poor beggars in red; guns

Vocabulary Builder, p. 94

A. Sample Answers

1. To *dominate* is to rule, control, or exert influence over someone or something. To *domineer* is to exercise arbitrary or overbearing control.

2. The *Dom* signifies a position of importance or influence, and implies that the person is a "master."

3. An *indomitable* enemy is one that cannot be overpowered or overcome, one that cannot be mastered.

B. 1. E; 2. A; 3. F; 4. D; 5. B; 6. C

Enrichment: Science, p. 96

1. Students' calculations of cumulative land loss for the additional years should yield these results:

Year 9: Point A-81; Point B-58.5

Year 11: Point A-99; Point B-71.5

Year 13: Point A-117; Point B-84.5

Year 15: Point A-135; Point B-97.5

2. Students may defend the protection of beaches as beneficial to people or animals and plants who use or inhabit the beaches. The protection of cliffs may seem less vital. Students may argue that the expense is too great, since the sea will wear away at human-made structures as well. Or they may argue "selective" protection depending on land use, type of protection required, expense, and so on.

Poems by Matthew Arnold and Rudyard Kipling

Open-Book Test, p. 97

Short Answer

1. The speaker's mood seems calm and peaceful. The poet uses phrases such as the following: "sea is calm," "moon lies fair," "tranquil bay," "sweet is the night air."
   Difficulty: *Easy*   **Objective:** *Literary Analysis*

2. The speaker appreciates the power of the sea. He feels the sea brings in a note of sadness, and the poet seems to understand the timelessness of the sea.
   Difficulty: *Average*   **Objective:** *Interpretation*

3. The speaker concludes that the world is troubled with conflict, struggle, and the decline of faith. He believes we must trust in one another because there is no other help or certainty. This conclusion may relate to the Victorian period, which witnessed many new discoveries that shook people's faith in traditional religious and social values. The Crimean War also caused concern.
   Difficulty: *Challenging*   **Objective:** *Reading*

4. The poem is specifically addressed to God, but the larger audience is the people of the British Empire.
   Difficulty: *Average*   **Objective:** *Interpretation*

5. The mood might be described as "forewarning" or "solemn," as the title of the poem indicates an end to something. Kipling sets a mood that portrays the greatness of the British Empire but also warns against such human follies as pride and arrogance.
   Difficulty: *Easy*   **Objective:** *Literary Analysis*

6. Kipling seems to admire and respect the British Empire, but he also recognizes the fallibility of humans who think they control the world around them. He recognizes that boastfulness is a dangerous trait that blinds people to reality.
   Difficulty: *Challenging*   **Objective:** *Reading*

7. The "widow" is Queen Victoria, as is indicated by references to her sons (soldiers, all men at the time) and to the "gold crown" on her head.
   Difficulty: *Easy*   **Objective:** *Interpretation*

8. Examples may include the dropped "h" sound and the repeated reference to poor beggars. The cockney accent suggests the perspective of the commoners and reinforces their plight, as the poem is written from that point of view.
   Difficulty: *Challenging*   **Objective:** *Interpretation*

9. As *tranquil* means peaceful or calm, you would feel peaceful.
   Difficulty: *Average*   **Objective:** *Vocabulary*

10. Mood details may include the following: pays poor beggars in red; barbarous wars; "all Creation she owns," "we've salted it down with our bones," "they'll never see 'ome." Theme: The commoners do not profit from the power and wealth of the Queen.
    Difficulty: *Average*   **Objective:** *Literary Analysis*

Essay

11. Students' essays should note the mood of sadness, struggle, and hopelessness that Arnold portrays, especially in the final stanzas of the poem. Their statement of theme should reflect this mood. Students should use quotes from the poem to support their answers.
    Difficulty: *Easy*   **Objective:** *Essay*

12. Students should note the tranquil, literal sea that is described in contrast to the troubled turmoil of the "Sea of Faith." Their conclusions should recognize and address this dichotomy.
    Difficulty: *Average*   **Objective:** *Essay*

13. Students' essays should note that both Arnold and Kipling have a dimmer view of the gilded age of Queen Victoria's reign than the view of most of their contemporaries, which touted the British Empire as a model of civilization. Students should use quotes from the poems to support their ideas.
    Difficulty: *Challenging*   **Objective:** *Essay*

14. Evaluate students' writing on clarity, corherence, and specific support. In their essays, students should refer

specifically to the elements listed: setting, mood, tone, and theme.

Difficulty: *Average*   **Objective:** *Essay*

Oral Response

15. Oral responses should be clear, well organized, and well supported by appropriate details from the selections.

Difficulty: *Average*   **Objective:** *Oral Interpretation*

ordinary people and that the glory of England will not last forever.

Difficulty: *Easy*
Objective: *Essay*

17. Evaluate students' writing on clarity, coherence, and specific support. In their essays, students should refer specifically to the elements listed: setting, mood, tone, and theme.

Selection Test A, p. 100

Critical Reading

1. ANS: C	DIF: Easy	OBJ: Interpretation
2. ANS: D	DIF: Easy	OBJ: Literary Analysis
3. ANS: A	DIF: Easy	OBJ: Reading Strategy
4. ANS: B	DIF: Easy	OBJ: Comprehension
5. ANS: D	DIF: Easy	OBJ: Comprehension
6. ANS: A	DIF: Easy	OBJ: Comprehension
7. ANS: C	DIF: Easy	OBJ: Interpretation
8. ANS: D	DIF: Easy	OBJ: Comprehension
9. ANS: C	DIF: Easy	OBJ: Reading Strategy
10. ANS: B	DIF: Easy	OBJ: Literary Analysis
11. ANS: B	DIF: Easy	OBJ: Reading Strategy

Vocabulary and Grammar

12. ANS: A	DIF: Easy	OBJ: Vocabulary
13. ANS: C	DIF: Easy	OBJ: Vocabulary
14. ANS: D	DIF: Easy	OBJ: Grammar

Essay

15. Students should mention that the main idea of the poem is the loneliness and misery of human life. The beach and the tide bring the misery of life to the speaker's mind as he listens to the tides sweeping forward and backward onto the beach. It is a melancholy sound that makes the speaker think of Sophocles and how he thought of the ebb and flow of human misery. The Sea of Faith makes the speaker recognize that few people have faith anymore. Only his love gives him hope.

Difficulty: *Easy*

Objective: *Essay*

16. Students may recognize that Kipling was proud of his country's achievements and a strong supporter of the empire. However, they will also recognize that Kipling's enthusiasm was tempered by caution. For example, in "Recessional," he compares Britain to ancient cities that are now known only to history. He knows that England's power will fade in time. Likewise, in "The Widow at Windsor," he recognizes that Britain's power is built upon the sacrifices of the soldiers and sailors who fight for Britain. So although he is proud of his nation's achievements, he is also aware that it was earned by the sacrifices of

Selection Test B, p. 103

Critical Reading

1. ANS: C	DIF: Average	OBJ: Comprehension
2. ANS: D	DIF: Easy	OBJ: Reading Strategy
3. ANS: B	DIF: Average	OBJ: Literary Analysis
4. ANS: C	DIF: Challenging	OBJ: Literary Analysis
5. ANS: D	DIF: Easy	OBJ: Comprehension
6. ANS: C	DIF: Average	OBJ: Interpretation
7. ANS: A	DIF: Challenging	OBJ: Literary Analysis
8. ANS: B	DIF: Easy	OBJ: Reading Strategy
9. ANS: D	DIF: Easy	OBJ: Comprehension
10. ANS: C	DIF: Average	OBJ: Reading Strategy
11. ANS: A	DIF: Easy	OBJ: Interpretation
12. ANS: D	DIF: Average	OBJ: Literary Analysis

Vocabulary and Grammar

13. ANS: A	DIF: Easy	OBJ: Vocabulary
14. ANS: C	DIF: Average	OBJ: Vocabulary
15. ANS: A	DIF: Easy	OBJ: Grammar
16. ANS: B	DIF: Average	OBJ: Grammar

Essay

17. Students should state that the message of the poem is a warning to nations as well as to people who hold power. The repeated phrase "Lest we forget" is a reminder that power and glory come at a price and are ultimately transient.

Difficulty: *Easy*

Objective: *Essay*

18. Students should acknowledge that although Kipling's poems include a message of caution, they are not anti-imperialist. The speaker in "Recessional" does not imply that having "dominion over palm and pine" is a bad thing. He just asks for guidance in that dominion. In "The Widow at Windsor," the speaker, a soldier, has a healthy respect for "Missis Victorier," although he also expresses a healthy dose of sarcasm about the job that she sends him out to do. He is not rebellious, though, just accepting of the reality of his lowly, dirty job for the sake of the Empire.

Difficulty: *Average*

Objective: *Essay*

19. Evaluate students' writing on clarity, coherence, and specific support. In their essays students should refer specifically to the elements listed: setting, mood, tone, and theme.

Primary Sources: "Progress in Personal Comfort" and Cook's Railroad Advertisement

Primary Sources Worksheet, p. 106

1. Smith logically compares modern comforts to life without them./ None

2. None/ round the world—the rail did not go all the way around the world.

3. None/ round the world—the rail did not go all the way around the world

4. Smith language appeals to emotions: "I groped around" "*my* hat has often been reduced to a pulp. .." and is humorous/ picture of well-dressed woman standing on top of the globe appeals to emotions—be on top of the world/ also is humorous.

5. smith is more logical but he also appeals to emotion. Cook's has no logic; it is only an appeal to emotions, using some deception and faulty reasoning.

Vocabulary Builder, p. 107

A. 1. fracture
2. Gout
3. macadam
4. privations
5. bilious
6. pulp
7. depredation

B. 1. G; 2. F; 3. E; 4. C; 5. D; 6. B; 7. A

Selection Test: Informational Texts, p. 108

"Progress in Personal Comfort" and Cook's Railroad Advertisement

Critical Reading

1. ANS: C	DIF: Easy	OBJ: Literary Analysis
2. ANS: B	DIF: Average	OBJ: Literary Analysis
3. ANS: C	DIF: Average	OBJ: Literary Analysis
4. ANS: D	DIF: Average	OBJ: Literary Analysis
5. ANS: C	DIF: Average	OBJ: Literary Analysis
6. ANS: A	DIF: Challenging	OBJ: Literary Analysis
7. ANS: B	DIF: Challenging	OBJ: Literary Analysis
8. ANS: C	DIF: Average	OBJ: Literary Analysis

Essay

9. Student answers will vary. Students may pick a technology—like the Internet—and write a persuasive essay that tells why it is good. They should address the arguments against it, as well.

Condensed version of Sample Answer: The advent of the Internet has been a giant leap forward for society. Now, in seconds, we can have any information at all at our fingertips. We can make airline reservations, research a medical condition, or communicate with a friend at the other end of the world. . . . Some may argue that because of the Internet, kids are no longer developing social skills. This is not true. . . .

Difficulty: *Average*
Objective: *Essay*

"Remembrance" by Emily Brontë
"The Darkling Thrush" and "Ah, Are You Digging on My Grave?" by Thomas Hardy

Vocabulary Warm-up Exercises, p. 111

A. 1. pulse
2. dreary
3. existence
4. bleak
5. canopy
6. shone
7. check
8. sternly

B. Sample Answers

1. Yes, Grandma's ring was a <u>cherished</u> family heirloom.
2. Yes, Bill <u>severed</u> contact with his neighborhood friends.
3. A dog shows <u>fidelity</u> to its master.
4. Winning a car would make me feel <u>ecstatic</u>
5. I had the flu once, and it left me feeling <u>frail</u>.
6. A paper cut only hurts a little, and so it would not cause me great <u>anguish</u>.
7. I was two when I was <u>weaned</u> from my baby blanket.

Reading Warm-up A, p. 112

Sample Answers

1. (rhythmically hitting her window); *Pulse* means "regular beating," or "throbbing."
2. (incessant beeping from the clock); *Check* means "to stop something."
3. As Carrie stepped out the door and into the <u>dismal</u>, rainy day, she had a smile on her face; Many people consider paperwork *dreary*.
4. (of clouds); A different kind of *canopy* would be one over a four-poster bed.
5. She started along her usual route, dodging puddles, dog walkers, and other determined runners who were <u>firmly</u> refusing to let the bad weather interfere with their daily exercise; A parent who is correcting a disobedient child may need to act *sternly*.
6. (This rainy atmosphere); A landscape without trees or grass can feel *bleak*.
7. (she was filled with tranquility); *Existence* means "life."

8. By the time she headed home, a weak sun <u>glowed</u> through the clouds; A gold ring *shone* through the window of the jewelry store.

Reading Warm-up B, p. 113

Sample Answers

1. (everyone in the family agreed they had never seen him so filled with joy); I would be *ecstatic* if I won a cruise.
2. (from its mother); A kitten would need to be *weaned* from the mother cat.
3. <u>rambunctious</u>, <u>rotund</u>, <u>enormous</u>; A piece of antique glass would probably be *frail*.
4. (much-loved); I *cherished* my first teddy bear for many years.
5. <u>loyalty</u>; I could demonstrate *fidelity* by standing up for a friend.
6. (heartbreaking); Our vacation on the tropical island was a complete <u>delight</u>.
7. (separated) (constant companionship); When a tree is being cut down, first the branches are *severed* from the trunk.
8. <u>impending</u>; My mother tried to *hasten* me out the door so that I would not miss the bus.

Literary Analysis: Stanza Structure and Irony, p. 114

Sample Answers

"Remembrance"

1. eight
2. four lines, with five feet in each, often starting with a trochee; *abab* rhyme scheme
3. The consistency of stanza structure makes the reader expect each stanza will focus on the same theme.
4. In stanza six, speaker explains that she has learned to live without her love.
5. The regular stanza structure leads the reader to expect that speaker will follow her love to the grave, when in fact, she decides to live.

"The Darkling Thrush"

1. four
2. eight alternating lines of four and three iambic feet, *abab cdcd* rhyme scheme
3. The consistent stanza structure creates the expectation that all stanzas will have the same gloomy mood and subject matter.
4. In stanza three, a bird sings a joyful song, which leads the speaker to concede in stanza four that there might be hope.
5. The reader is lulled into complacency by the singsong quality of the stanzas, only to be surprised, as the speaker is, by the thrush's hopeful song.

"Ah, Are You Digging on My Grave?"

1. six
2. six lines of four feet each, except the second and the last, which have three; *abcccb* rhyme scheme
3. Reader expects a question and answer in each stanza; the repeated question also builds suspense.
4. In stanza four, reader learns the digger is not, like the others asked, a human being, but is the speaker's dog. In stanza six, the dog states that he has also forgotten his mistress.
5. The speaker and reader both expect the digger will care for the speaker. Also, the serious subject matter now becomes darkly humorous.

Reading Strategy: Read Stanzas as Units of Meaning, p. 115

A. Sample Answers

1. The speaker describes how she has grieved for her love, who has been dead for fifteen years.
2. In stanzas six through eight, the speaker realizes that she cannot spend her life grieving and that she has learned to live without her love.
3. In each stanza, the speaker guesses who is digging on her grave, and the digger answers. Each answer conveys the idea that a person is forgotten after death.

B. Sample Answers

Stanza 1: Images create a desolate mood.

Stanza 2: Death seems to surround the speaker.

Stanza 3: A frail bird sings a joyful song.

Stanza 4: The bird knows a reason for hope of which the speaker is unaware.

Overall Meaning: Even in the bleakest of situations, one can find hope.

Vocabulary Builder, p. 116

A. 1. D; 2. E; 3. A; 4. B; 5. C
B. 1. rapturous; 2. gaunt; 3. prodding; 4. obscured; 5. languish; 6. terrestrial
C. 1. obscure; 2. gaunt; 3. rapturous

Grammar and Style: Using Active Voice, p. 117

Sample Answers

Dear Ms. Satchel,

I enjoyed your history class this semester. In fact, I think all of your students enjoyed the class. Your sense of humor created liveliness and a great atmosphere in the classroom. I have never enjoyed history until now. Your teaching brought it alive for me. I am sad because the year is ending.

I envy your future students. Have a great summer!
Your student,
Nigel

Enrichment: Naturalism, p. 119

1. B; 2. A; 3. D; 4. C

Poems by Emily Brontë and Thomas Hardy

Open-Book Test, p. 120

Short Answer

1. a world without a loved one, therefore a world without love. Because the speaker has lost the person so loved, he or she has determined not to seek love again.
   Difficulty: *Easy* **Objective:** *Interpretation*

2. Brontë uses quatrains, or rhyming, four-line stanzas.
   Difficulty: *Easy* **Objective:** *Literary Analysis*

3. Students may note patterns such as the first and third stanzas, which begin "Cold in the earth . . ."; the first, second, third, and last stanzas, which end with questions; or the nouns that are capitalized, such as Time, World, Despair, and Memory. The patterns emphasize ideas and feelings that the speaker is expressing, and they also set the reader up for the final thought of the poem.
   Difficulty: *Challenging* **Objective:** *Literary Analysis*

4. Students may suggest that the speaker perceives winter as dreary, based on words and phrases such as "frost was specter-gray," "dregs made desolate," "shrunken hard and dry," "fervorless," and "bleak."
   Difficulty: *Average* **Objective:** *Interpretation*

5. The rhyming pattern is *ababcdcd* in each stanza. The poem's repetitive rhyme strongly suggests the sameness and monotony of the bleak winter mood, so that the introduction of the thrush in the third stanza is a surprise to readers.
   Difficulty: *Challenging* **Objective:** *Literary Analysis*

6. The poem ends ironically when the speaker alludes to the thrush's "blessed Hope" and then uses understatement to describe it as an emotion of which he was "unaware."
   Difficulty: *Average* **Objective:** *Literary Analysis*

7. The digger is the dead speaker's pet dog. The dog is at the grave because he wants to bury a bone there.
   Difficulty: *Average* **Objective:** *Interpretation*

8. Stanza 1: the speaker wonders if the digger is her loved one; Stanza 2: the speaker wonders if the digger is one of her kin; Stanza 3: the speaker wonders if the digger is an enemy; Stanza 4: the speaker discovers that the digger is her dog; Stanza 5: the speaker rejoices at the fidelity of her pet; Stanza 6: the speaker discovers that the dog was simply burying a bone. The irony is that the dog, like everyone else, is simply going about its daily business with no thought of the deceased speaker.
   Difficulty: *Average* **Objective:** *Reading*

9. The speaker wants to be remembered and wants to know who is acknowledging her grave.
   Difficulty: *Challenging* **Objective:** *Interpretation*

10. As *rapturous* means extremely happy, you would be happy.
    Difficulty: *Average* **Objective:** *Vocabulary*

Essay

11. Students should note that the poems all create irony by developing stanzas that lead the reader to expect a certain ending. Then, in the final stanza, the poet unexpectedly gives a twist to the meaning the reader has been anticipating. For example, in "Ah, Are You Digging on My Grave?" the first stanza tells the reader that the speaker's beloved has forgotten her. The next stanzas reveal that the speaker has been forgotten by her relatives and enemies. Then, the dog is identified, and the speaker is relieved to learn that her best friend has remembered her. The final stanza surprises the reader with the unexpected discovery that the dog has forgotten her, too.
    Difficulty: *Easy* **Objective:** *Essay*

12. In their essays, students may explore the despair of "Remembrance," the juxtaposition of optimism with pessimism in "The Darkling Thrush," or the irony of "Ah, Are You Digging on My Grave?"
    Difficulty: *Average* **Objective:** *Essay*

13. In their essays, students should address the literal and symbolic aspects of the titles in relation to the meanings of the poems.
    Difficulty: *Challenging* **Objective:** *Essay*

14. Evaluate students' essays on clarity, coherence, and specific support. In general, students may point out that the specific settings of the Hardy poem function in an especially evocative fashion.
    Difficulty: *Average* **Objective:** *Essay*

Oral Response

15. Oral responses should be clear, well organized, and well supported by appropriate details from the selections.
    Difficulty: *Average* **Objective:** *Oral Interpretation*

Selection Test A, p. 123

Critical Reading

1. ANS: C	DIF: Easy	OBJ: Comprehension
2. ANS: A	DIF: Easy	OBJ: Reading Strategy
3. ANS: D	DIF: Easy	OBJ: Comprehension
4. ANS: C	DIF: Easy	OBJ: Literary Analysis
5. ANS: A	DIF: Easy	OBJ: Interpretation
6. ANS: D	DIF: Easy	OBJ: Interpretation
7. ANS: C	DIF: Easy	OBJ: Comprehension
8. ANS: A	DIF: Easy	OBJ: Interpretation

9. ANS: A	DIF: Easy	OBJ: Reading Strategy
10. ANS: D	DIF: Easy	OBJ: Literary Analysis

Vocabulary and Grammar

11. ANS: C	DIF: Easy	OBJ: Vocabulary
12. ANS: D	DIF: Easy	OBJ: Vocabulary
13. ANS: B	DIF: Easy	OBJ: Grammar
14. ANS: D	DIF: Easy	OBJ: Grammar

Essay

15. Students should note that the poems all create irony by developing stanzas that lead the reader to expect a certain ending. Then, in the final stanza, the poet unexpectedly gives a twist to the meaning the reader has been anticipating. For example, in "Ah, Are You Digging on My Grave?" the first stanza tells the reader that the speaker's beloved has forgotten her. The next stanzas tell that the speaker has been forgotten by her relatives and enemies. Then, the dog is identified, and the speaker is relieved to know that her best friend has remembered her. The final stanza surprises the reader with the unexpected discovery that the dog has forgotten her, too.

    Difficulty: *Easy*
    Objective: *Essay*

16. Students should give reasons for their response. For example, they may find "The Darkling Thrush" the most positive and uplifting of the three, and they may point out that the hope expressed by the aged thrush on the harsh, winter day is a positive, uplifting statement about how life ought to be lived.

    Difficulty: *Easy*
    Objective: *Essay*

17. Answers will vary. Students should select one of the poems and discuss how the author created a sense of place and then discuss what the original place must have been like. Sample: In "Ah, Are You Digging on My Grave?" the author creates a cold, dark place. The woman is dead and in her grave. She cannot see. She cannot tell what is going on and sees only in her imagination. The place allows sound, for she hears the dog's digging. The place that inspired the poem must have been the cemetery with all of its gravestones and the author's imagination—what must it feel like to be under the ground?

Selection Test B, p. 125

Critical Reading

1. ANS: C	DIF: Average	OBJ: Comprehension
2. ANS: A	DIF: Average	OBJ: Reading Strategy
3. ANS: B	DIF: Average	OBJ: Literary Analysis
4. ANS: C	DIF: Average	OBJ: Interpretation
5. ANS: A	DIF: Easy	OBJ: Comprehension
6. ANS: B	DIF: Average	OBJ: Interpretation

7. ANS: D	DIF: Easy	OBJ: Literary Analysis
8. ANS: B	DIF: Average	OBJ: Interpretation
9. ANS: C	DIF: Average	OBJ: Reading Strategy
10. ANS: D	DIF: Easy	OBJ: Comprehension
11. ANS: B	DIF: Average	OBJ: Reading Strategy
12. ANS: A	DIF: Average	OBJ: Literary Analysis

Vocabulary and Grammar

13. ANS: C	DIF: Average	OBJ: Vocabulary
14. ANS: A	DIF: Easy	OBJ: Vocabulary
15. ANS: B	DIF: Average	OBJ: Vocabulary
16. ANS: C	DIF: Average	OBJ: Grammar
17. ANS: D	DIF: Easy	OBJ: Grammar

Essay

18. Students should recognize that each stanza conveys an idea or creates a mood. The first stanza of "The Darkling Thrush," for example, sets the mood for the poem, and subsequent stanzas reinforce the mood. Students should also see the stanzas as parts of a whole. For instance, the individual stanzas of "Remembrance" describe the speaker's struggle with her loss; when taken as a whole, the stanzas convey the deeper meaning of the poem: Life cannot be lived in a state of constant grieving.

    Difficulty: *Easy*
    Objective: *Essay*

19. Students might contend that Brontë's poem is atypical of Romanticism. While it begins with a rush of strong emotion, the poem ends with the speaker's resignation toward her loss. "The Darkling Thrush" seems more Romantic than Naturalistic; the final mood of the poem is cautiously optimistic, with the speaker daring to hope that the new century will usher in good rather than ill will. However, "Ah, Are You Digging on My Grave?" is a good representation of Hardy's naturalistic beliefs; he refuses to give in to the sentimentality that the speaker professes.

    Difficulty: *Challenging*
    Objective: *Essay*

20. Answers will vary. Students should select one of the poems and discuss how the author created a sense of place and then discuss what the original place must have been like. Students should compare the places. Sample: In "Ah, Are You Digging on My Grave?" the author creates a cold, dark place. The woman is dead and in her grave. She cannot see. She cannot tell what is going on and sees only in her imagination. The place allows sound, for she hears the dog's digging. The place that inspired the poem must have been the cemetery with all of its gravestones and the author's imagination—what must it feel like to be under the ground? The actual place would have been sunny and bright with a dog digging in the grass surrounding the tombstones while the literary place is dark and lonely.

"God's Grandeur" and **"Spring and Fall: To a Young Child"** by Gerard Manley Hopkins
"To an Athlete Dying Young" and **"When I Was One-and-Twenty"** by A. E. Housman

Vocabulary Warm-up Exercises, p. 130

A. 1. seared
2. flame
3. smudge
4. shod
5. trod
6. smeared
7. toil
8. fleet

B. Sample Answers
1. The writer's <u>renown</u> was obvious since *everyone* had heard of her.
2. "I shall feel <u>rue</u> that I ever met you," the lady said to the *villain she hated.*
3. She <u>outran</u> her teammates and came in *first.*
4. The <u>grieving</u> man was *filled with tears and sadness.*
5. The <u>blight</u> on the roses made them look *withered and sick.*
6. Children <u>flock</u> happily to *a carnival or circus.*
7. Books he read *over and over* were the filmmaker's <u>springs</u> of inspiration.

Reading Warm-up A, p. 131

Sample Answers
1. (thickly coated); You might see tar being *smeared* on a driveway.
2. (a large flame); *Seared* means "burned on the surface."
3. (burning the feet); *Shod* means "to be wearing shoes."
4. (on foot); You might *trod* through an open field or a marsh.
5. (dirty smoke); A *smudge* can often be found near a door handle or on a window sill.
6. (when lighted); I've seen a bonfire *flame.*
7. (extracting the wax from the bayberries was a tedious process); Digging a trench for a pipe requires a lot of <u>toil.</u>
8. (quickly went out of fashion); *Fleet* means "rapid."

Reading Warm-up B, p. 132

Sample Answers
1. (magnificent gesture); A gesture that has *grandeur* might be an official granting amnesty to people who are political prisoners.
2. <u>fame</u>; A great accomplishment or invention could bring someone *renown.*
3. (regrets); Many now have regrets and <u>sorrow</u> when they remember the day that Scheifflin made this sentimental gesture.
4. <u>native birds began dying off rapidly</u>; You might find people *grieving* at a funeral service.

5. (together by the hundreds or even the thousands, filling trees and darkening the sky); People who want to hear an outdoor concert might *flock* to the park where it is being held.
6. <u>speedily</u>; A person who did more work than was expected *outran* the expectations that were placed upon him.
7. (pests); Bird lovers considered starlings a *blight* because the starlings interfered with the health and growth of other birds.
8. <u>inspiration</u>; The inspiration or <u>origins</u> of Scheifflin's idea may or may not have been self-serving, but the result wasn't the peaceful integration of species that he had intended.

Literary Analysis: Rhythm and Meter, p. 133

Sample Answers
1. Today, the road all runners come,
   iambic tetrameter
   Shoulder-high we bring you home,
   trochaic tetrameter
   And set you at your threshold down,
   iambic tetrameter
   Townsman of a stiller town.
   trochaic tetrameter
2. And for all this, nature is never spent:
   There lives the dearest freshness deep down things;
   1st line: *counterpoint rhythm*
   2nd line: *iambic pentameter*

Students may observe that the meter gives the words dramatic expressiveness and contributes to the mood of a poem.

Reading Strategy: Apply Biography, p. 134

Sample Answers
Hopkins
Trait: belief in uniqueness of all things; "There lives the dearest freshness deep down things;" ("God's Grandeur," line 10)
Trait: love of nature; the image of "worlds of wanwood leafmeal" ("Spring and Fall," lines 2, 8)
Housman
Trait: studied Greek and Latin; reference to laurel wreath, a classical Greek symbol for an athlete's victory ("To an Athlete Dying Young," line 25)
Trait: bitterness; There is bitterness as well as humor in the lines "And I am two-and-twenty, / And oh, 'tis true, 'tis true." ("When I Was One-and-Twenty," lines 15–16)

Vocabulary Builder, p. 135

A. Sample Answers
1. duckdelight, splashbeggar, socksoaker
2. leafpromises, summerhopes, the first sun-eager leaf buds of spring

3. the puppies tumbletripped to the food dish, their rasptongues scraped my cheek

4. sunsprawling metal-antheap; childbursts

B. 1. A; 2. C; 3. D 4. C; 5. A; 6. D

Support For Writing: Letter of Recommendation, p. 136

1. Sprung Rhythm: All feet begin with a stressed syllable and contain a varying number of unstressed syllables/ Examples: from "Spring and Fall: To a Young Child": Margaret are you grieving / over Golden Grove unleaving/ Hopkins uses sprung rhythm, which gives his poems their complexity. The lines are densely stressed with many echoing consonant and vowel sounds.

2. Inscape: Hopkins's idea that there was a uniqueness in all things that he called a precious individuality. This is present in all his poems in how he describes everything as precious and beautiful./ Example: "God's Grandeur": The World is charged with the grandeur of God/ It will flame out, like shining from shook foil./ His awe in all things causes the reader to appreciate things he or she may not think about in ordinary life.

3. Coined words: Use of existing words to create new ones./ Examples: unleaving; wanwood; leafmeal/ Fresh, unique language that allows the reader a fresh perspective.

Enrichment: Social Studies, p. 137

Sample Answers

1. A straight northwest route will take this traveler from London to the small town in Worcestershire where Housman was born. From there, go straight east to Cambridge, where Housman taught Latin.

2. This traveler should head northwest from London to Liverpool, on the coast. From there, continue north and slightly northwest to Glasgow, Scotland.

3. This traveler should first make a short hop to the northeast to Stratford, Essex—Hopkins's birthplace. Then, a trip to the northwest will take the traveler to Housman's birthplace in Worcestershire.

4. Both poets studied in Oxford, which is a fairly short trip to the northwest from London.

5. Travelers might go northwest to northern Wales, then across the Irish Sea by ferry to Dublin.

Poems by Gerard Manley Hopkins and A. E. Housman

Open-Book Test, p. 138

Short Answer

1. The poem focuses on God the Creator of all nature, and there is a specific reference to the Holy Ghost.

Difficulty: *Easy*   **Objective:** *Reading*

2. Sunrise is a spectacular example of the sensory grandeur that Hopkins describes in the poem and attributes to the handiwork of God.

Difficulty: *Average*   **Objective:** *Interpretation*

3. Sample answer: Students may describe the grandeur of the world, the freshness of nature, or the sunset and sunrise described in lines 11–12.

Difficulty: *Challenging*   **Objective:** *Reading*

4. Hopkins wants all of the feet of the poem to begin with a stressed syllable, thus creating "sprung rhythm."

Difficulty: *Average*   **Objective:** *Literary Analysis*

5. Spring and fall and their contrast are symbolic of childhood and adulthood and the contrast between those times of life.

Difficulty: *Challenging*   **Objective:** *Interpretation*

6. By dying young, the athlete will never lose his glory. The athlete's death will memorialize his glory as the victor in a race; if he aged after winning the race, others would undoubtedly surpass his achievement or replace him in the townspeople's minds.

Difficulty: *Average*   **Objective:** *Interpretation*

7. The poem is written in tetrameter, with four feet per line. Lines 3, 6, and 8 are trochaic.

Difficulty: *Average*   **Objective:** *Literary Analysis*

8. The word "given" must be treated as one syllable in order to keep the established rhythm of iambic trimeter.

Difficulty: *Average*   **Objective:** *Literary Analysis*

9. Students' charts should show that in the first stanza, the speaker is told not to give away his or her heart; in the second stanza, the speaker is told not to be sorry about having given away his or her heart—it is never a vain act. Students' answers on reconciling the two pieces of advice will vary, but they should recognize that the poem contains a paradox.

Difficulty: *Challenging*   **Objective:** *Interpretation*

10. The harvest would probably not be good, since *blight* means "a condition of withering."

Difficulty: *Average*   **Objective:** *Vocabulary*

Essay

11. Students should note that the speaker in "Spring and Fall: To a Young Child" is addressing Margaret, a child. The speaker in "To an Athlete Dying Young" is addressing an athlete who has just died. In "To an Athlete Dying Young," the speaker tells the athlete that he is better off having died young before his record was broken. In "Spring and Fall," the speaker tells Margaret that sadness about leaves falling will lessen as she grows older and sees how all things die. The speaker's position is weakened, however, by the observation that Margaret herself will die and it is in fact herself that she

really mourns. Students may decide that neither speaker's sympathy is entirely convincing.

Difficulty: *Easy*   **Objective:** *Essay*

12. Students should recognize the emphasis that the rhythm places on ideas and also how the unpredictability of the rhythm reflects the unpredictability of nature and the world in general.

Difficulty: *Average*   **Objective:** *Essay*

13. Students' personal levels of connection to the poem's meaning will determine their responses. Essays should be supported with examples from the poem.

Difficulty: *Challenging*   **Objective:** *Essay*

14. Responses will vary, although many students will see Hopkins as the more innovative writer, especially with regard to formal elements. Evaluate students' essays on clarity, coherence, and specific support.

Difficulty: *Average*   **Objective:** *Essay*

Oral Response

15. Oral responses should be clear, well organized, and well supported by appropriate details from the selections.

Difficulty: *Average*   **Objective:** *Oral Interpretation*

Selection Test A, p. 141

Critical Reading

1. ANS: B	DIF: Easy	OBJ: Reading Strategy
2. ANS: D	DIF: Easy	OBJ: Interpretation
3. ANS: C	DIF: Easy	OBJ: Literary Analysis
4. ANS: C	DIF: Easy	OBJ: Comprehension
5. ANS: B	DIF: Easy	OBJ: Interpretation
6. ANS: A	DIF: Easy	OBJ: Literary Analysis
7. ANS: C	DIF: Easy	OBJ: Interpretation
8. ANS: A	DIF: Easy	OBJ: Comprehension
9. ANS: D	DIF: Easy	OBJ: Literary Analysis

Vocabulary and Grammar

10. ANS: C	DIF: Easy	OBJ: Vocabulary
11. ANS: D	DIF: Easy	OBJ: Grammar
12. ANS: A	DIF: Easy	OBJ: Vocabulary
13. ANS: B	DIF: Easy	OBJ: Vocabulary
14. ANS: C	DIF: Easy	OBJ: Grammar

Essay

15. Students should note that the speaker in "Spring and Fall" is addressing Margaret, a child. The speaker in "To an Athlete Dying Young" is addressing an athlete who has just died. Both speakers attempt to comfort their listeners. In "To an Athlete Dying Young," the speaker tells the athlete that he is better off having died young before his record was broken. In "Spring and Fall," the speaker tells Margaret that sadness about leaves falling will lessen as she grows older and sees how all things die.

The speaker's position is weakened, however, by the observation that Margaret herself will die and it is in fact herself that she really mourns. Students may decide that neither speaker's sympathy is entirely convincing.

Difficulty: *Easy*

Objective: *Essay*

16. Students should mention that Hopkins has an intense love of nature. He states his feelings most obviously in "God's Grandeur," in which he describes the world as "charged" with the grandeur of God. In "Spring and Fall," Hopkins is more sympathetic toward humans. He describes the beauty of the natural world and the sorrow of Margaret as she witnesses the falling of leaves. Then, he concludes that people are part of nature and will die, as all living things do.

Difficulty: *Easy*

Objective: *Essay*

17. Responses will vary, although many students will identify Hopkins as the more innovative writer. Students should support their answer about who is the more innovative writer and give reasons why they prefer one style over the other.

Selection Test B, p. 146

Critical Reading

1. ANS: B	DIF: Average	OBJ: Comprehension
2. ANS: B	DIF: Average	OBJ: Literary Analysis
3. ANS: C	DIF: Average	OBJ: Literary Analysis
4. ANS: A	DIF: Easy	OBJ: Reading Strategy
5. ANS: C	DIF: Average	OBJ: Comprehension
6. ANS: B	DIF: Average	OBJ: Interpretation
7. ANS: D	DIF: Challenging	OBJ: Reading Strategy
8. ANS: A	DIF: Average	OBJ: Interpretation
9. ANS: B	DIF: Easy	OBJ: Interpretation
10. ANS: A	DIF: Easy	OBJ: Interpretation
11. ANS: C	DIF: Easy	OBJ: Literary Analysis

Vocabulary and Grammar

12. ANS: D	DIF: Easy	OBJ: Vocabulary
13. ANS: D	DIF: Average	OBJ: Vocabulary
14. ANS: A	DIF: Average	OBJ: Vocabulary
15. ANS: C	DIF: Average	OBJ: Vocabulary
16. ANS: C	DIF: Average	OBJ: Vocabulary
17. ANS: A	DIF: Average	OBJ: Vocabulary

Essay

18. Student essays should reflect the understanding that Housman has chosen an athlete to represent humanity at the pinnacle of positive experience in the world. An athlete represents this height in the following ways: Athletic victory is visible and measurable, and all recognize victory in athletic competition. Athletic competition

is limited in scope, so its successes are clear-cut. The virtues of athletes are measured only by their skill. Athletes are generally regarded as attractive, young, and strong. All these qualities symbolize humanity at the summit of its optimism, and it is from these heights that years drag us down.

Difficulty: *Easy*

Objective: *Essay*

19. Students should recognize that Hopkins clearly regards humanity as a spoiler of the beauty of nature, not a part of it. In "God's Grandeur," he explicitly states that "men do not now" understand, that "all is seared with trade; bleared, smeared with toil; and wears man's smudge and shares man's smell" and even humanity's feet do not feel "being shod." This may represent humankind's fallen state as dictated by Hopkins' theology, which is implicitly expressed in "Spring and Fall: To a Young Child." The child as she grows will "come to such sights colder" "nor spare a sigh" at the destruction of nature. This is the "blight man was born for." Hopkins sees humans not in the natural landscape, but outside it, and apart from it, and as unworthy of its beauty.

Difficulty: *Average*

Objective: *Essay*

20. Responses will vary, although many students will identify Hopkins as the more innovative writer. Students should support their answer about who is the more innovative writer and give reasons why they prefer one style over the other.

Writing About Literature—Unit 5

Analyze Literary Periods: Integrating Grammar Skills, p. 147

Sample Revisions

1. Matthew Arnold lamented the decline of religious faith and protested the rise of materialism. Because he worried about educational standards, he worked to improve English schools. The effects of the Industrial Revolution and the rise of British imperialism were two other social changes that concerned him.

2. Although Rudyard Kipling supported British imperialism, he also recognized the dangers of overblown national pride. He warned the British people that their status in the world would not last forever. The British empire would come to an end some day.

3. When the Irish potato crop failed in 1845, the Irish people began to starve. More than a million Irish people died of starvation and disease, and even more emigrated, especially to the United States. The British, trying to improve the Irish economy, took land away from small farmers and encouraged larger, more efficient farms. Instead of improving the crisis, though, this move made the famine worse.

4. When Charles Dickens's father was sent to debtor's prison, Dickens was forced to work in a factory as a boy. These experiences inspired Dickens to write novels of

social criticism, but his novels are also full of delightful characters and suspenseful plots. Critics have praised the depth of his understanding of human nature. Generations of readers have simply fallen in love with his plots and characters.

Writing Workshop—Unit 5

Research Report: Integrating Grammar Skills, p. 148

Charles Dickens made two trips to North America. The first was in 1842, when Dickens traveled with his wife to the United States and Canada. Although the journey was successful, Dickens created controversy by supporting the abolition of slavery. Later in the trip, Dickens spent time in New York City. There he gave lectures and raised support for copyright laws. In addition, he recorded many of his impressions of America. During his one-month stay, he met famous American authors such as Washington Irving and William Cullen Bryant.

Dickens made his next trip to the United States in 1867. He spent most of this trip in New York. During his tour, he gave 22 readings at Steinway Hall and four at Plymouth Church of the Pilgrims. He also wrote about many significant changes he observed in the United States. His final appearance was at a banquet at Delmonico's in 1868. There he promised to never criticize America again. Shortly thereafter, on April 23, 1868, Dickens boarded his ship to return to Britain.

Vocabulary Workshop—5, p. 150

A. 1. This movie is lifeless, with a sluggish pace and tedious plot.

2. Bring up that topic again and you will be wasting our time with something that we have already covered completely.

3. If he loses his job, he will be in serious danger of disaster.

4. They remained together when life was easy and when it became difficult.

5. Who makes the decisions in that family?

B. Suggested answer:

Everyone assumed that he had absolutely no chance to win the election. Most of the political insiders did not want to be closely associated with him. However, he emerged from the financial scandal with his reputation completely undamaged. They had firmly believed that his career was over, but they were so fixed on the details that they did not pay attention to the larger issues.

Benchmark Test 9, p. 152

MULTIPLE CHOICE

1. ANS: B

2. ANS: C

3. ANS: B
4. ANS: D
5. ANS: A
6. ANS: B
7. ANS: D
8. ANS: B
9. ANS: B
10. ANS: B
11. ANS: A
12. ANS: D
13. ANS: B
14. ANS: B
15. ANS: D
16. ANS: B
17. ANS: D
18. ANS: B
19. ANS: A
20. ANS: C
21. ANS: A
22. ANS: C
23. ANS: A
24. ANS: A
25. ANS: B
26. ANS: C
27. ANS: D

ESSAY

28. Students should accurately identify aspects of the writer's life and works and show the relationship between them. Their essays should demonstrate their ability to narrate a sequence of events and identify events that relate to the writer's works.

29. Students' recommendations should demonstrate their knowledge of the poet's life and work and should include details that support their point of view.

30. Students should discuss specific social issues addressed in specific works of fiction. They should discuss the role fiction played in making the public aware of those issues and changing relevant attitudes and practices.